Shudda, Cudda, Wudda

SHUDDA, CUDDA, WUDDA

Affirmations to Cope with Self-Doubt

A.J. Chevalier, Ph.D.

Health Communications, Inc.
Deerfield Beach, Florida

©1996 A.J. Chevalier
ISBN 1-55874-387-1

Publisher: Health Communications, Inc.
          3201 S.W. 15th Street
          Deerfield Beach, Florida 33442-8190

Cover design by Nancy Kim Graves '

to my parents
and
the Spirit
that overcomes

The Stronghold

To those who would mourn
   the loss of my life
   let them know
   that I found it again
Never was it really lost
   just stuck inside
   a mass of thoughts
     and feelings
   and worn-out actions
   all judged in a harsh way
By looking within
I found it again.
The Stronghold
   of ME
   is the beat of my own heart
   and all the earth echoes
   that ring in like manner

The Stronghold

The Stronghold is the beat
  of my own heart
  and all rhythms
  that ring in like manner.

ajc
1995

Introduction

Let me introduce you to the voices in my head: Shudda, Cudda and Wudda. Do you know them? Have you heard them once or twice? In my life they have been constant companions, ever-present commentators on the experiences of my days. They have in an odd way become like family. They won't go away, their voices and their influences have been long-lasting—that is, until now.

I decided to confront these three voices and discover the place of power I had given them in my life. They were willing to come for a talk as long as they could appear together. They tell me they are "old friends." I agreed to meet them head-on if I could bring an important friend as well.

So let me introduce you to all these friends—the voices in my head—and see if you already know them. As we settle in for this discussion, I find comfort once again in knowing the power of confronting my own fears. As the three "old friends" settle in, I now look to the places I have given them in the decisions I make and the consequences I face.

Shudda is Dr. Shudda B. Ashamed, professor of style and all that is proper. She has devoted her very existence to the study of how things must be done. In her mind there is one *right* way, and she knows it. She sits on every committee that makes decisions. She studies all that is proper, keeps track of it and offers her expertise whether it is asked for or not.

Further, Shudda sits in a rigid manner, her bluish hair in a tight bun and her lips pursed. She is eternally vigilant, waiting her turn to tell anyone how to do something—anything. Looking over her spectacles at all things that annoy her, she is the master of the gift of guilt. She carries guilt in her purse, in her shoes and in every nook and cranny on her person. Guilt is the gift she gives freely to all. Her job and responsibility is to let me know where I fall short.

With her, there is little discussion about how to do things because she knows all things. She spouts her wisdom in a shrill, ear-piercing tone. The only way to stop her is to agree with her. She then settles into a sing-song version that is almost soft and sweet, and she tells me that my agreement with her will save my neck one more time.

The giver of guilt is on duty 24 hours a day, taking no time off unless relieved by the voice I know as Cudda. Dr. Cudda Tried-harder is a longtime companion of Shudda. They relieve each other from time to time as commentators on all I do. Dr. Cudda Tried-harder is a character, too.

Cudda is the architect of "can't do" and hopelessness. Cudda can be seen in his white doctor's coat, wringing his hands with worry, pacing the floor and finding the best of excuses for all my actions. Constantly on the alert and thinking, he has provided me with star-studded excuses for anything and everything at a moment's notice. He is the Wizard of "why."

Cudda oversees the part of my thinking that convinces others that all my actions make sense if they just know my reasons. He is in charge of reasons. For years a student of how and why things happen, he now has the job of spotting scary things while they are still miles away and bringing them up close, "so we can get ready for the worst now." In his chair, he sits forward, wringing his hands, and posing the worst of all possible outcomes, no matter what the situation.

He is the die-hard of disaster. He attempts to be ready for everything and he misses nothing. He goes over and over all events that happen to me and presents these to me even as I am falling asleep from exhaustion from a normal day's work. His last murmur as I drift off to the safety of sleep is, "Don't worry, I'll wake you when *they* come to get you." Passing out, I hear him say, "What if . . . what if . . . what if?"

He never rests and is always there as soon

as I wake up each day. The prince of panic, he whispers, "Something is already wrong today—you just don't know what it is yet. Stay tuned. I'll keep you informed." A great friend of Shudda, he is devoted to helping me find my way around in all my relationships.

The trio is complete with the voice I know as Wudda. Dr. Wudda Ifonly is a longtime friend of Shudda and Cudda. Wudda prefers to begin each day angry and then try to find another way to be. But as each day lingers on, he finds more and more to be angry about. He is quick to spot injustice of any kind and in any measure. His reactions are sudden and unpredictable. He holds a hammer for swatting flies.

He loves to discuss injustice with anyone who will listen. He, like the others, is constantly on the alert and tells me this is a must—for my own safety. He believes that anything we cannot foresee we cannot handle. He is convinced that everyone is waiting their turn to crap on us, and he is in charge of heading off "crap."

Staying angry, he tells me, keeps him on his toes. "I'm always looking for the hand that would do us in," he says. He tells me to be grateful that he at least cares and is on guard, on my behalf. "Crap is everywhere," he says. He *knows* when "shit will happen."

Like his ability to see and snap at injustice, he is equally capable at finding just the "right" person to use to justify our actions. He convinces me quite often that another person is responsible for my actions. Something they did or said sparked a needed reaction of his, which he pitches to me and I use.

He says we could always get more done if "so and so" wasn't in our way. "Someone," he says, "is always in our way." He has found a couple of ways out of this one, though. He has appointed himself manager of my hopes and dreams. As manager, he finds all "accurate" reasons for not going ahead with my dreams.

His judgment about such dreams is that they border on the impossible and they require too much stretching to reach them. He declines help from others, preferring instead to do things alone and in his own way.

He is often deep in thought about why things aren't working and how others have made life difficult for me. Like Cudda and often Shudda, he sees no way out. There is just long-suffering.

Do you know them? Ever heard their voices in your head? If you haven't or if you have, makes no difference, they say. They are here to instruct and tell us how our lives are to be lived.

That is not exactly *my* purpose, however. I am more interested in figuring out what I have let them do to me over the years. I think they mean well, but at the same time, they help me to reject responsibility for my own actions.

If I do not look at their influence, I fear that my life will be given to phantom thoughts and imagined misery. I might find miserable things to do with my time. These back-seat drivers and doctors of self-doubt send me spinning for answers from anyone but me. The result is a life lacking joy, peace and purpose.

Shudda, Cudda and Wudda have formed a committee of misgivings and are consultants of all hindsight advice. They put an old spin on anything I do and as the "spin doctors" of the daily events in my life, inflict self-doubt and indecision upon all I do.

Alongside of them has popped up another voice, the voice of Dr. Ima WiseOne. She softly offers encouragement when I ask for it and am willing to listen. She knows of my humanness and cherishes all that it means to be human. She is thoroughly familiar with all my talents and capabilities. She loves to watch me as I face any situation in my life.

She fears nothing and knows the Source of All That Is. She tells me that she is from the All That Is—THE SOURCE, and that she has been assigned to reassure me in this lifetime. She asks me to accept my own humanness. Quite simply, she loves me no matter what.

I have asked her to attend this meeting of the minds. As she approaches, the other three are stunned by the sense of calm power that surrounds her. She is dressed in comfortable denim, a favorite T-shirt and tennis shoes. Her voice is smooth and inviting, and she is at home with herself and with me.

She sits behind me and puts the palms of her hands gently on each of my shoulders and whispers, "It is a good thing that all of us are here. We will get to the bottom of all this in a good way. You will know once and for all that you have all you need to know. You will know that you *are* now all you need to be. And you can trust that."

With a gentle touch to my shoulders and amid the grumbling from the committee of misery, she whispers, "Begin."

ajc
Buffalo, Wyoming

JANUARY

Is there ever
really a wrong turn?
Or do we face lessons
at each bend in
the journey?

At about 11 P.M. on this day, I found myself wishing I had devoted my time to painting.

Shudda: You should learn how to use your time more wisely, eh?

Cudda: And you could have if you had started earlier in the day.

Wudda: You would have been able to do that painting if your husband had awakened you earlier, don't you know?

IMAWISE: All things considered, it was really a lovely day because you loosened your agenda enough to breathe on this first day of the new year.

NEW THOUGHT

What I plan and how I plan are decisions
I make based on the knowledge
I have at the time.

I forgot to write out my resolutions for the new year and at about noon today, I thought of changes I need to make.

Shudda: Things done right are things done on time, little girl.

Cudda: Yes ma'am, how true, how true. You can't do things without a plan.

Wudda: This life feels impossible unless you have the right plan and you can do it all on your own. Now that's impressive!

IMAWISE: There are days that are well spent without a plan and then there is also a time to plan. No hurry on either.

NEW THOUGHT

When I need a plan, I make one that really fits me. My life has need of unplanned and planned times.

January 3

Someone stepped on my feelings this day, and I left the office angrier than a hornet.

Shudda: Now, now, dear, anger is not an acceptable response. What would others say if they saw you angry?

Cudda: What if they say you lose your cool? Then what would happen to you?

Wudda: You would lose all you worked for and hope for, that's what! Anger is an impossible emotion. Stifle it!

IMAWISE: Anger lets you know you are hurt or disappointed, and it is natural. You can lose your cool and get over it.

NEW THOUGHT

When I am angry, I can see myself as
a normal human being having a
normal human experience.

At 10:30 A.M. this day I was late, and the day seemed over. I woke up too late to do anything about it.

Shudda: Setting one's alarm clock is always the best plan. Then check and double check it the night before.

Cudda: And if you can't do it right, your clock needs to be replaced right away. Lousy clock!

Wudda: Well, it's really unfair that you have to rely on that piece of crap! Maybe you can rise with the sun without a clock and that way you will never be late again!

IMAWISE: Occasionally, situations such as this occur in everybody's life. If you take it in stride, so will everyone around you. Decide what you need to do next.

NEW THOUGHT

When I make mistakes, I know I have the right to do so. I own them and move on with my life.

I was running late again as I had done the previous morning. I moved too slowly and ended up leaving a few minutes later than I should have, in a huff about how the day began.

Shudda: If you had listened to me, time would not have been a problem. Set that clock, girlie, and check it twice.

Cudda: What's the worst that could happen here? Get fired?

Wudda: How many times has the boss been late? Yeah, now ask him that and then see what he says. . . . You have a right to know that, you know!

IMAWISE: There are some days when everyone simply moves more slowly, and I am here to tell you that includes you.

NEW THOUGHT

I move about at the pace that is right for me and I make no excuses. I accept responsibility for my actions.

Why haven't I found a support group to help me with my eating habits? I gain and then I lose too much weight.

Shudda: Three basic meals a day, that's what I always say. Nothing will do you better than three good ones a day.

Cudda: What if you eat the wrong things and then you get cancer or something like that? You could, you know!

Wudda: You ought to be able to lose on your own, without anyone's help. If you take help from somebody else, it won't do any good. You'll lose and gain, lose and gain.

IMAWISE: Ask yourself what you would really like for yourself and then take reasonable and practical action to get it.

NEW THOUGHT

I can take action right now to move
in the direction I want for my health, and
I can do the rest one step at a time.

Instead of worrying about the outcome of leaving my office early, I probably needed to tell folks where I was going. I was not sure they would understand.

Shudda: You are in trouble no matter where you are when you break the rules.

Cudda: You did it because they were not able to understand and you were afraid of their disapproval. Most understandable, my dear.

Wudda: You can't tell others about your personal business. They just won't be there for you, that's for sure.

IMAWISE: When you have a need, you can determine who else needs to know about it and live with the consequences of your actions.

NEW THOUGHT

I have a right to privacy about my own
needs. I know when to share
these needs with others.

When I attended an art show on this day, I felt sad when I left the building. I wished I had studied art.

Shudda: You should be ashamed. Just look at how much schooling you do have and the jobs you have had. Uh-uh, missy. . . .

Cudda: If you even think about that out loud, you will lose the job you have. Others are jealous, you know.

Wudda: You are too old now to start over, so if you have to do it, make it a hobby.

IMAWISE: You can start over anytime you want. You can do many things in your life. The choice is yours.

NEW THOUGHT

I start today, this minute, on the dream of
my choice. Nothing propels me
further than my own dream.

Even as an adult, I still feel others question my motives, and so I often ask for permission. This day I asked permission to hunt for my own supplies in our office.

Shudda: Now that's playing by the rules, little girl. Good for you!

Cudda: What if the people you work with think you are weak?

Wudda: You should tell them you need your own supplies, and to get them for you right now!

IMAWISE: Trying to understand other people's boundaries is a tricky thing. It is okay to make mistakes when trying to understand where you begin and others end.

NEW THOUGHT

I take note of what feels right to protect
my boundaries. I can live through
what happens as a result.

I proposed a new plan at the office today. I developed it on my own and presented it to the people I work with. They were surprised at my work.

Shudda: What are you trying to do—show how smart you are or something? What do you think that will get you?

Cudda: Tell 'em you had nothing better to do and it was just a little effort in the right direction.

Wudda: Things are impossible at that office anyway. If they don't like it or want to help you with it, just scrap the whole thing! Got it?

IMAWISE: When you have a new idea or new plan, you can decide upon the proper time and way to share it. Others' reactions cannot be controlled, so you can let go of trying to control them.

NEW THOUGHT

I enjoy my new thoughts and what I am able to develop. I trust my judgment.

11

This day I spoke up at work about some obvious employment problems and practices. I was the only one to speak up, while others sat silently.

Shudda: Good thing I caught you before you said too much. They were after your hide.

Cudda: Now what if you lose your job? Then what will you do?

Wudda: There are some days when you have to keep quiet, no matter how bad things get.

IMAWISE: Speaking up is often the only thing that feels right. The results may be something you do not like. You can live through those, too.

NEW THOUGHT

Sometimes my voice is the voice of reason, long forgotten and set aside by others.

When someone recently misjudged my work, I stood up for myself, defending what I had done.

Shudda: There is one right way to do things, you know, and you should be glad I am here to fix things when you step out of line.

Cudda: Changing others is hopeless and there's nothing you can do to change what they think.

Wudda: Other people are usually not working as hard as you are, anyway.

IMAWISE: There are many ways to do things and by explaining your way, you present an opportunity for others to learn.

NEW THOUGHT

I can talk about what I do calmly
and still get my point across.

I quit a job without much notice. I followed the store policy but it still seemed hurried to me.

Shudda: There are proper ways to do things and when you don't follow them, there are real problems.

Cudda: They are probably going to make it hard for you to get work anywhere else in this state, you know.

Wudda: Why is it that you always get the short end of the stick? Not fair!

IMAWISE: There are times when all you can do is the best you can do. When you have decided that you have done your best, you can rest.

NEW THOUGHT

My best is all I ever can do.
When I have done that I can relax.

When I had the chance this day, I spoke up for myself in a difficult situation: caught between two friends.

Shudda: You should have been nicer to those who need you. "Others first," you know!

Cudda: And you could have done that, but if you had, you'd lose at least one of them as a friend—maybe both; probably both.

Wudda: If they had just left you alone, there would have been no problem in the first place, but no—they had to start something they couldn't finish.

IMAWISE: You will know when and how to speak for yourself. The words you need come to you when you need them.

NEW THOUGHT

It is my right to speak up and
I am capable of finding
the right words.

I've left high-paying jobs in pursuit of my dreams—things I felt I had to do in this lifetime.

Shudda: Now if you had listened to me, you would know that you need security to make you feel okay.

Cudda: You could have found your dream or something close enough to it right where you were. Now you've really done it.

Wudda: Just try to find it yourself, right where you are and you'll be okay; you don't need anyone else's help.

IMAWISE: Pursuing a dream is no more dangerous than anything else. Everything you do is simply a lesson.

NEW THOUGHT

I know in my heart what is right for
me to do and I can do it
one step at a time.

When I try to make big changes, I always think I need to go for counseling, and then I often find a way out of asking others for help.

Shudda: You should know better than to expect someone else to help you. Help yourself!

Cudda: That's it—do it yourself. If you involve other people they'll only want you to do it their way.

Wudda: When you have to get help you also have to take a lot of crap from others. Better to do it alone!

IMAWISE: Often, asking for help is a wise thing to do. When you think of doing it and actually do it, it is the right and best time for you.

NEW THOUGHT

I can trust myself to know when to ask
for help and when I can make
changes by myself.

If I had a better start in life, I would have come to what I really wanted to do much sooner. This thought makes me mad and sad.

Shudda: You should have listened to your mother when she offered her advice on getting a job.

Cudda: You could have been a star by now, but you went the way you thought was best. See what thinking does!

Wudda: If your parents had asked you what you wanted and you had told them, you wouldn't be here today.

IMAWISE: A "better" start might have meant different experiences, not necessarily "better" ones. The start you had is the one you needed to get where you are today.

NEW THOUGHT

What can I take from all my experiences that helps me today? I have learned a great deal from what has already happened to me.

18

I look at my skin and my body and always wish I had taken better care of myself, exercised more, eaten the right foods and downed eight glasses of water each day.

Shudda: Yes, look at you now. Your body has simply given over to the rules of gravity, and you know what gravity does!

Cudda: Think of all the times you could have worked out or eaten better. You probably are well on your way to cancer or some other disease!

Wudda: You really had it rough as a child and even as a young person, so you only understood a little about how to take care of yourself. Others should have shown you.

IMAWISE: You can appreciate where you are today and love your body. You are a spiritual being in human form. Any habits you want to change, you can change.

NEW THOUGHT

I decide what is proper care for my body.
I can make choices that fit my needs.

I remember the time I devoted to being a step-parent and found myself wishing that I was a better parent.

Shudda: You should always put the kids first. They are God's blessing to you.

Cudda: How could you think of yourself when you have children? Pretty selfish!

Wudda: What you hoped to gain by your own dreams vanishes right before your eyes if you forget those who really need you.

IMAWISE: You did the best you could with the light you had at the moment. All of us do. That is all we can do.

NEW THOUGHT

When I do the best I can, that is all I can really do. I am the one who needs to accept that.

At a very important meeting I was asked to explain some of my actions on behalf of the people I serve.

Shudda: You must put a high priority on having others understand what you are doing. Do not leave them hanging.

Cudda: Pay attention to what worries you, and you will work harder to help others understand you.

Wudda: Well, you can't act so high and mighty that you cut others out of what you are trying to do. They can't get it because you are trying to talk above them.

IMAWISE: When you explain your actions, talk in a calm way about your choices. Take time to feel pride in your work.

NEW THOUGHT

I can leave defensive feelings out of my interactions with others when I remember that I have done my best.

When I was angry, I needed to walk away. Instead, I probably said too much—something I now regret.

Shudda: Now see here, raising your voice gets you nowhere fast. And then you can't take it back.

Cudda: Like toothpaste out of the tube, lava out of the volcano, now you've done it! Look out—for the fallout!

Wudda: Now if you had listened to me, I would have told you these people you are with are impossible morons and could not understand you if they had to.

IMAWISE: Anger is a human emotion common to everyone. You have the right to your own anger and the ability to make amends.

NEW THOUGHT

When I get angry, I remember that this
is human. As a human, I make
mistakes and amends.

Trust has always been hard for me, no matter what relationship I am involved in.

Shudda: You need to trust more. Trust and obey, that's what I say.

Cudda: When will you learn? How old will you be before you can have relationships with good people?

Wudda: I would remind you that when you do get in a relationship, you do not pick so well.

IMAWISE: Get to know the reasons why it is hard for you to trust, and then decide to do something about them.

NEW THOUGHT

When I try to understand myself,
I find good reasons for my own behavior.
I can change what I need to change.

Others were being hurt and so was I, and I acted like nothing was happening for a long time.

Shudda: Shhh! Keep quiet! You do not know for sure what others are doing.

Cudda: Speaking up for injustice is a hopeless cause and always ends up hurting you.

Wudda: Hopes and dreams of making a difference—that's all they are—just hopes and dreams!

IMAWISE: When you let yourself know what you really value, you find the stuff you are really made of. You also find pride in yourself.

NEW THOUGHT

I find within myself the rules to guide my life
that make sense to me.
My own principles free me.

I spoke up about the injustice that I witnessed toward others and thought that by speaking up, I could do something about it. I found I was ignored.

Shudda: See, that's what you get for speaking up when no one asked you to.

Cudda: What's your excuse this time? Playing the martyr role?

Wudda: Well, now you see what others are really made of, don't you? They could care less about what you think, anyway.

IMAWISE: Speaking up about suffering and injustice is a personal choice, guided by principle. You know when to speak up.

NEW THOUGHT

It is my choice to speak up and
I am able to handle all that comes with it.
I know the right times to speak up.

January 25

As a grown person, I often feel far from my childhood years. Sometimes I think if I just loved my family more, our relationship would somehow be better.

Shudda: Now, now, dearie, family is first. Honor your parents and all those you love.

Cudda: And because you didn't, you are heading for some of life's saddest moments and most difficult times.

Wudda: You have really made those relationships impossible now and there's nothing that can be done to improve them.

IMAWISE: That was then and this is now. You did what you had to do and you can try again if you feel it is best. A relationship works when two people try.

NEW THOUGHT

What I did was all I knew how to do.
I can choose to make amends and to develop
the kind of relationships I want.

I watched a friend suffer through a terrible marriage, one in which she was forgotten repeatedly and treated very harshly.

Shudda: Go take her by the hand and show her the way out of her troubles. There is only *one* way out and you know it.

Cudda: It's up to you, and you only, to lighten her load. What kind of friend are you if you don't help her?

Wudda: Only you know what she needs to overcome her sense of hopelessness.

IMAWISE: Sometimes the best help we can offer others is to let them come to their own solutions. When you suffered, you learned better ways to take care of yourself.

NEW THOUGHT

I do not always have to jump in and do
for others in need. There are times when it is
good to stay on the sidelines and let
others figure out what they need.

When I first became aware that my needs were very different from those of most of the people I knew, I thought there was something wrong with me. Then I felt I should have paid more attention to those needs.

Shudda: You have to follow the rules of meeting other people's needs first.

Cudda: There were thousands of reasons why you couldn't attend to your own needs. No one ever taught you to do that.

Wudda: If you are honest about your needs, someone will crap on you and then what?

IMAWISE: You do know your own needs when you listen to yourself in any situation. You can tend to your own needs and let others tend to their own.

NEW THOUGHT

It is safe to consider my own needs
no matter what situation I am in. It is my
right and my responsibility.

Before I left my first marriage and two stepchildren, I gave much thought to the effect that my leaving would have on them. I found myself wishing I had spent more time with them so they would understand my actions.

Shudda: Now see, that's what gets you into trouble: leaving your *real* responsibilities.

Cudda: You could've stuck it out if they really meant anything to you.

Wudda: What you chose to do landed you in an impossible situation, which, quite frankly, you deserve.

IMAWISE: You did what you could on behalf of the children in that relationship. You have both good and not so good times to remember about that period of your life.

NEW THOUGHT

I learn as much from what I call my mistakes as I do from success. Each is an important lesson for me and for those around me.

I began this day growling and found later some incredible understanding from my partner. I know that I should have been nicer to him.

Shudda: People can leave you when you don't act right toward them.

Cudda: What if he leaves now and you never see him again?

Wudda: I know I would leave if you talked to me that way. You only have one chance to do it right, you know.

IMAWISE: The way you begin the day is not the way you have to finish it. At any moment you can start over.

NEW THOUGHT

Making amends when I wrong
someone else is my chance to start over.
That is a choice I have at
any moment.

On a wintry day, I dressed for a much warmer day and came down with a sudden cold.

Shudda: See, that's all it takes. Now you know better than to dress for the tropics.

Cudda: You made your bed, so to speak, and now you know what you can do.

Wudda: If it were up to me, I'd ask the bosses to turn up the heat, but they probably wouldn't because of the cut in funds. You'll just have to accept the conditions that made you sick.

IMAWISE: There is a powerful lesson of self-care and self-love to be learned here. What parts of your body need warmth and care?

NEW THOUGHT

My first consideration is proper care of my body. I know how and when to do that.

I could have tried to be more understanding of other people's needs, even when what they were doing was really hurting me. I set myself aside to help them and found myself angry the whole time.

Shudda: Others, yes, others: let this my motto be!

Cudda: If you don't put others first they will quit being your friends, and they will find a way to hurt you badly.

Wudda: If I were you, I'd really think about that. It is sometimes just impossible to say "No."

IMAWISE: Saying "No" is your choice. You can tend to your own needs in spite of what is happening around you.

NEW THOUGHT

The single best thing I can do for myself
is to learn when to say "No,"
and mean it.

FEBRUARY

One so-called
"right" way may lead
to all kinds of
detours, exits and
wrong ways.

February 1

I left for dinner not thinking that I should call my girlfriend who was about to have her third child. I was to be there when this one came into the world. I should have called earlier.

Shudda: There you go again, putting your little needs before anyone else's.

Cudda: What if she was feeling lonely? She will never have anything to do with you again.

Wudda: There go your hopes of being comfortable here with friends in this small town.

IMAWISE: Did you do the best you could do at the time? A second question might also help: What do you believe about yourself and your mistakes?

NEW THOUGHT

I am entitled to mistakes. I am the
one who allows this for myself.

A snowstorm sneaked over the nearby mountain pass. Taking the back road home was neither a good nor safe idea. Whiteout conditions prevailed and I knew I should have taken the interstate.

Shudda: That you should have known because people talk about whiteouts all the time here.

Cudda: Now what will you do? What can you do? You are the worst snow driver I've ever seen! You'll slide off the mountain!

Wudda: This is absolutely impossible. Now look at what you've done!

IMAWISE: This is your chance to show what you can do to make yourself safe. You remember the rules you taught yourself for driving in snowy conditions.

NEW THOUGHT

I know now what I need to
do to face my fear.

Everywhere I go I find that I trust too much. I have this childlike belief that everyone is good and kind and cares about everyone else. I rarely enter a new situation thinking about the possibility of poor motives on anyone's part.

Shudda: You must always be on the lookout for people who do things the right way and those who are, shall we say, "different."

Cudda: You could have looked for them the whole time and never seen them.

Wudda: If you had trusted less, you wouldn't have as much crap as you have on you right now.

IMAWISE: Entering each new situation as a child is not such a bad thing. Just don't look for your mother everywhere.

NEW THOUGHT

I enter new situations in a way that helps me think good thoughts. I can handle the reality of situations I face.

I am learning to step aside and let others learn what they need to learn or refuse to learn it. The last day of work as a therapist, I visited with one client who complained better than anyone I ever met. She told me all the reasons why she couldn't do her own healing.

Shudda: You should step in to help others when you know more than they do.

Cudda: This could have been different for her if you had only helped her more.

Wudda: What would it have taken out of you—to open yourself one last time?

IMAWISE: We all need to learn when to stop. It is a good lesson.

NEW THOUGHT

I can feel good about stopping
when I feel it's appropriate.

I often regret that I could not do more for my family as a child. As a child, I felt like an adult and now as an adult, I often feel like a wounded child, wishing the life of my parents could have been different for them.

Shudda: You should have thought about that at the time, young lady.

Cudda: You could have been a better kid and helped more around the house.

Wudda: What about all that yelling you did? You know it got to them.

IMAWISE: When a child, be a child. You were not responsible for the tasks of adulthood. Once an adult, be an adult and remember the child within.

NEW THOUGHT

I am both the adult I see and the
child I feel inside today.

I knew my family needed some kind of help, and I put that idea so far out of mind that I forgot what hurt any of us. From that point of view, I found it easy to drown in pain. I could have asked that we all go in for help.

Shudda: You should know better, dearie. You really can't save everybody, but you might have tried.

Cudda: You just couldn't get them all together—impossible, simply impossible!

Wudda: The reason this would never have worked is that they all would have made fun of you.

IMAWISE: Knowing your family needs help and getting it for them are two very different things. Children need help to get some things done.

NEW THOUGHT

What I want and what I am able to do
are often two different things.

After too many hours of work, I slumped into the nearest comfortable chair. For one brief moment, I felt my own exhaustion. I let down all airs and felt a new feeling of being totally tired.

Shudda: There's not time for that. Time's a wastin'. Get to it, sweetie!

Cudda: The reason you are so tired has to do with what *they've* put on you.

Wudda: If you rest now, the situation will worsen and there will be no way out.

IMAWISE: Exhaustion is a very clear clue to your next step. It tells you exactly what to do.

NEW THOUGHT

I let myself be tired when I *am* tired and
I take care of that need right away.

I pride myself on always doing my part. I usually do much more than my part. I am so dependable that others can leave their parts, go away, and when they come back, their parts will be done.

Shudda: You can do their work in half the time; what's the difference?

Cudda: People come to expect that of you and when you don't come through, the worst is sure to happen.

Wudda: They want you to do their work so that they can do whatever they want to do.

IMAWISE: The role you find for yourself is big enough in any situation. Allow others to find their own roles.

NEW THOUGHT

I know that playing my role is
enough in any situation.

I am learning how to let others learn their own lessons in whatever way they choose, and then to let the chips fall where they may. I was beginning to find peace in doing this, when I saw how a friend could be completely ruined by the actions he was about to take.

Shudda: It is your job to step in when people are about to fail.

Cudda: If his situation is hopeless, there is nothing you can do but worry with him.

Wudda: He should be able to pull himself up by his own bootstraps. Any man would do that.

IMAWISE: First, take care of yourself in any event you face. Others may not learn what they need to learn unless you get out of their way.

NEW THOUGHT

When I take care of myself and let
others do the same, that is
enough work for all.

I knew as a consultant that I was correct about my assessment of several problems I encountered with the host agency. I found that my words fell into a black hole and were ignored.

Shudda: You should have talked them into the right way.

Cudda: If you had, you could be free of worry, but as it is, I think you deserve to worry.

Wudda: There go all your dreams because when you are wrong, someone in authority will get wind of it and be comin' after you.

IMAWISE: If you offered your best assessment and advice, then that is all you can do.

NEW THOUGHT

I can ask myself in any situation,
"Have I done all that I can do?"
If so, I can let it go.

In an attempt to explain something to those who hired me, I found that no one understood what I was saying. I tried several times in several ways. Still, no one "got" it.

Shudda: There is a way to explain things and a way *not* to explain things.

Cudda: They couldn't get it because you didn't find the right way.

Wudda: There's no way out of this situation, just no way at all!

IMAWISE: People don't understand each other all the time. If Hitler and Billy Graham both understood you and liked your message, you might wonder about your message. . . .

NEW THOUGHT

I am responsible only for doing the best job I can do. The rest is up to others.

One recent weekend filled up with activity before I could stop it. It seemed that both days were sunk into activities for everyone I knew. The end of that weekend was the first time I felt I had time to take a breath.

Shudda: You should stay busy! Idle hands are the devil's workshop!

Cudda: If you haven't a full day for yourself, you haven't lived to the fullest.

Wudda: Even if no one else helps you, you need to stay busy helping those you care about.

IMAWISE: Filled time is not necessarily quality time. Quiet, "unbusy" time is essential for good health.

NEW THOUGHT

Busy or free, my time is
directed by my needs.

I could save so much money by shopping with coupons, and yet I almost always lose or forget them. Five or six dollars more are spent each time I shop.

Shudda: You should keep coupons with you at all times and check them daily.

Cudda: You could start earlier to collect them and then put them in an obvious place at home.

Wudda: If family members did not take so much of your time, you would remember things like this.

IMAWISE: There are many techniques to use to jog your memory. Try different ways till you find those that work for you.

NEW THOUGHT

I try new ways to organize my life.

When I was a stepmother, I did a lot of the thinking for my kids. I looked for their answers while they waited on the sideline. Then they resisted my help and resented my answers.

Shudda: Children need someone to think for them! How else are they going to learn?

Cudda: What if you let them alone and they just fumble themselves into real trouble?

Wudda: They can't do it for themselves because they don't have the experience you have.

IMAWISE: Your kids also saw that you acted from your heart. They saw someone who was really trying to help.

NEW THOUGHT

I can allow others to make their own choices and learn from them as they live out the consequences of their decisions.

February 15

All the car wrecks I have had tell me one thing. I need to pay more attention to traffic signals every time I drive. Always in a hurry, I never slow down to a pace that allows me to follow the rules.

Shudda: That's how accidents happen, and you certainly have caused your share.

Cudda: I, for one, do not believe you are capable of leaving on time for anything.

Wudda: Most traffic lights stay red for too long anyway. If nobody's coming, what's the difference?

IMAWISE: The difference can mean life or death. Slowing down won't kill you; driving too fast just might.

NEW THOUGHT

I can slow down and take
life as it comes.

When my path took me down an unexpected road and I made some drastic new choices, I lost several friends who did not agree with my choices. I felt that I had befriended them and then they walked out on me.

Shudda: What you get out of a relationship is what you put into it.

Cudda: You could have picked other friends or helped these friends understand what you were doing.

Wudda: I think it is better to do things alone. Anyway, who needs 'em?

IMAWISE: You are always in charge of your choices and can learn to live with the consequences that arise from them.

NEW THOUGHT

I make choices based on my understanding of the situation at hand. I choose to feel good when I take full responsibility for my choices.

February 17

On frigid mornings here in Wyoming, I need to warm up the car before blasting off in it. I rarely do, however, and still do not appreciate the consequence of driving with a cold engine. I ask someone else, usually my husband, to take care of my car.

Shudda: If you own something, you should take care of it.

Cudda: If you don't, God will take it away from you.

Wudda: I know for a fact that you have to do it all yourself or it won't get done.

IMAWISE: Any choice is a lesson, and some are more expensive than others.

NEW THOUGHT

I learn from each choice I make.

In all my years as an adult, I have probably balanced my checking account three times. I always knew when I could spend no more. I could count on my intuition.

Shudda: You should balance your checkbook all the time and know to the penny the state of your finances.

Cudda: You could have done it all along if you had taken the time.

Wudda: You would have done it sooner if your parents had cared to show you how.

IMAWISE: As an adult you can still learn anything you need to learn.

NEW THOUGHT

When I need to learn how to do something now, I ask for help and learn from others.

February 19

Upon moving to a new community, I could find no work in my field. I took a job in a gift shop, which reminded me of my high school work days. I often felt bad that I was doing something far below my educational level.

Shudda: You made bad choices that took you back to your high school days.

Cudda: You've really gone downhill now—heading for the worst that is yet to come.

Wudda: Well, what do you know? All those hopes and dreams right into the toilet. Told you!

IMAWISE: Starting over and performing a day's work are both honorable tasks.

NEW THOUGHT

There are times when starting over
is the best choice to make.

A cry for help from a good friend led me to the phone. She had called so many times, interrupting anything and everything that went on in my house. With my new family, I found that I wanted some private "family" time.

Shudda: You can do for her and for the family. The "right" thing is to do for others.

Cudda: If you had asked her to call later, then you could have taken care of her too.

Wudda: You can only put so many limits on what others are to do.

IMAWISE: Boundaries and limits are important for any person to set.

NEW THOUGHT

The limits that I have in my family
are legitimate. I am the only one who can
help others respect my limits.

I often wish that I had received encouragement in the arts as a child. No one in my family seemed plugged into them. I learned to make an art of helping, but harbored a secret desire to learn something in the visual arts.

Shudda: You should be grateful for what you had. Your family gave you their appreciation of the arts.

Cudda: You'll just have to learn to appreciate what you have.

Wudda: It is impossible to turn back the hands of time. You have lived with it this far, so get on with it.

IMAWISE: You can still learn whatever you want to learn.

NEW THOUGHT

What I wanted to learn may have been
blocked before. I can choose
to learn at any age.

In the midst of some real craziness, I found an incredible inner wish to find something good to say. From my point of view, there was really nothing good to say about the situation, and yet I longed to smooth it over.

Shudda: People really appreciate it when you can find something good to say.

Cudda: You could put the hope back into a hopeless situation.

Wudda: Sometimes you are the only person who can do this, you know?

IMAWISE: There are times when saying something good in a bad situation means you are being dishonest.

NEW THOUGHT

I can offer my true opinion of any situation and deal with the results of my choice.

February 23

For my most recent work project, I could have done more and yet I felt that I was not up to it. In all projects past, I had served well and beyond my stated role.

Shudda: You should pull your own weight and help others who cannot help themselves.

Cudda: What if everybody did what you did?

Wudda: Then where would you be—where would we all be? What if the whole country did what you did?

IMAWISE: There are times when you are not up to doing something. This is natural, normal and, on occasion, expected.

NEW THOUGHT

There are times when I have enough energy and there are times when I require rest.

One woman called to say how miserable she was, living with her alcoholic son. She complained for nearly 15 minutes before I found a good question to ask, one that actually might help her.

Shudda: What took you so long? This woman needed help right away and you just kept her waiting.

Cudda: People have to get things off their chests and you know that, having been a counselor and a recovering person.

Wudda: I hope you told her how to get out of it; otherwise she will feel you are being unfair by holding back on the answers.

IMAWISE: Sometimes others can learn a lot from misery. They may see a need to make a change.

NEW THOUGHT

I can be with others in their pain
without living it for them.

When I disagree with others, I am learning the power behind the slogan, "Live and let live." Sometimes, however, I think others really need to know what I know, and I try to convince them of this. They resist and resent me, and I feel angry.

Shudda: You should know by now that you have to give of yourself when it is asked of you. You must share what you know.

Cudda: You could let them know that you are just too busy to get involved with them.

Wudda: If you want something done right, you have to do it yourself.

IMAWISE: When you live and let live, you free yourself and others.

NEW THOUGHT

I can learn to live without
judging others.

Having to say "No" has prompted me to feel automatic guilt for as long as I can remember. Recently, someone asked me to do something that I just couldn't bring myself to do. I said "No"—sort of.

Shudda: If you say "No," there needs to be a good reason that everyone can understand.

Cudda: There are times when you just can't say "No" and it is hopeless at those times to try.

Wudda: If you say "No," others will ask, "Why?" So be ready with a good answer.

IMAWISE: People hear "No" much of the time. You can choose to say "No" when it fits, and also choose whether you will explain the reason for your refusal.

NEW THOUGHT

Saying "No" is my personal right.
I can say "No" with or without explanation.

I recently heard of some serious problems that my professional expertise required. I spoke comfortably about possible solutions. The listeners heard the words and continued to complain that nothing would change.

Shudda: You should wait until others come to you for help. I have told you about being forceful. . . .

Cudda: They didn't listen because they were jealous of what you knew, so they had to ignore you.

Wudda: There's a good reason why they don't really want things to change. Here you go trying to change them!

IMAWISE: Every situation does not require your help. You can choose when you will offer help.

NEW THOUGHT

When I hear that someone needs help,
I can choose if, when and how
I want to be involved.

During a recent conflict with a loved one, I spouted off before I could catch myself. I was shocked at the sound of my own voice and the hateful words I used to describe how I felt. I later wished my tone of voice had been different.

Shudda: Wash your own mouth with soap! I've told you over and over that angry words never get you anywhere.

Cudda: What if everybody acted the same way you acted?

Wudda: You know, too, that your loved ones show anger the way you do and that's where you learned, eh?

IMAWISE: Remember that forgiveness works for most mistakes.

NEW THOUGHT

I am entitled to my own anger as it comes up in me. I can make amends for the mistakes I've made with others.

February 29

I faced a terrible ethical conflict and lingered over the matter probably longer than I needed to do. I just couldn't be sure of the right thing to do. I think now that I should have confronted the person earlier.

Shudda: If you speak your mind early on, you clear the way for doing the right thing.

Cudda: You have never been good at that because no one listened to you as a child, so why do you think they'll listen to you now?

Wudda: If you do speak up, they won't listen, and you will see that there are always reasons that things can't be done.

IMAWISE: You can take the time you need to make decisions in any situation you face. Being in a hurry is often an illusion.

NEW THOUGHT

I will take the time I need to determine
a right course of action.

MARCH

Pushing against
the wind leads to
much resistance,
flack and general
paranoia.

March 1

This morning in my office was a busy time. I went about my usual routine and then later decided I should have made more calls about my own work and art.

Shudda: I guess you think people will just swarm at the door for what you write and create.

Cudda: You could have started earlier, and that would have made the difference.

Wudda: There's really no one to help you—this one you have to do alone.

IMAWISE: One thing you can do to make the most of your time is prioritize what you are going to do for the day.

NEW THOUGHT

I set realistic priorities for each day and
feel good about what I accomplish.

I see some difficult dilemmas in the work I do in therapy. Part of what I did today was to shed light on those difficulties so that solutions could be found. Still, in the end, after all that hard work, I found that in some cases, I needed to be more convincing.

Shudda: Should have listened to me! I told you that they were not with you because you did not show them "the way."

Cudda: If they can't find "the way," then their lives are pretty hopeless and you've added to their sense of hopelessness.

Wudda: Ah, yes, their hopes and dreams become impossible!

IMAWISE: Everyone finds his or her own way among the rubble in each person's life. People need companions, not guides, along the way.

NEW THOUGHT

I find my own way and accompany
a few others who do the same.

It seems I have the idea that my body is not the right size now, nor has it ever been. I have dieted and lost and regained according to what is going on in my life. The picture of the person I want to be is always someone other than whom I see in the mirror.

Shudda: The very idea of looking in a magazine for the perfect body! Exercise! Exercise! Exercise! Eat three square meals!

Cudda: You could have drunk water every day for the last 20 some years, and your skin and your body would be the same.

Wudda: But no, diets and what others think don't really help now, do they? You have to do this alone, too.

IMAWISE: It makes sense to love your body into health no matter what shape you are in.

NEW THOUGHT

I love and appreciate my body just the way it is. I can make the changes I want.

I knew many years ago what I wanted to do. I stayed so far away from it. I don't really think that I have wasted my life; I just wish I had prepared myself to do other things.

Shudda: Now, don't you feel bad about how you've had what you wanted all along? And now, my dear, you don't want what you have?

Cudda: So you could have been someone else, huh? What about all the time and effort we put into guiding you in the right directions?

Wudda: There were reasons you couldn't get things done the exact way you wanted; there was no help from the parents, eh?

IMAWISE: You can take a lesson from that time and trust yourself more today.

NEW THOUGHT

Trusting myself today is a
moment-to-moment decision.

I loved the idea that I could earn money and buy just about anything I wanted. I learned that at age 11, when I went to work for the first time. Something got a hold of me then and I have never felt like I had enough of anything. I felt most alive when I was spending money.

Shudda: The love of money is the root of all evil. You should spend only if you really need something.

Cudda: What if you spent all the money you made each time you made it—then what?

Wudda: I would, if I were you, put it all in savings and never touch it. Rainy days come all too often!

IMAWISE: You need to establish a healthy relationship with money.

NEW THOUGHT

I can learn to have a new and healthy relationship with money.

I wait to ask for help until the very last minute, when I can no longer stand to try alone. I offer help to others at the first indication of their need for it. It seems very hard to give that to myself.

Shudda: There is a way to ask for help and a way not to ask for help.

Cudda: If you wait too long, there won't be any help left for you.

Wudda: You don't really need all that much help; most of what you need to do, you can do alone.

IMAWISE: Asking for help when you need it is a healthy thing to do.

NEW THOUGHT

I expect that from time to time, I will
need help. I am healthy and
normal when I ask for it.

There were many people who told me that I had the best job and that I would be crazy to leave it. They looked down their noses at the very sight of the dream I wanted to live and scoffed at my idea of wanting something more. I began to feel that I needed to stay put.

Shudda: At your age, why must you try things that are so dangerous? Think about retirement and security.

Cudda: What if you are at retirement age and there is no money? What will you do then?

Wudda: Social Security is already bankrupt, so there's no hope there. Better stash that dream of yours if it costs money, honey!

IMAWISE: Choices carry lessons, and all lessons can be learned.

NEW THOUGHT

Living my dream is simply a choice
I make and a set of lessons
I choose to learn.

I worked tirelessly on a recent project. I thought about it day and night—even dreamed about it. I kept refining the final product until I could find nothing else to do with it. Then I presented it to the person who commissioned it. He set it aside and ignored it for weeks.

Shudda: You should know that not everyone will appreciate what you do, no matter how much effort you put into it.

Cudda: You need to be concerned that he sees how hard you worked on this, so keep trying to show him.

Wudda: I would have told him that to begin with, and then I would have reminded myself that no one ever appreciates me enough.

IMAWISE: When you appreciate your own efforts fully, no one else has to do it for you.

NEW THOUGHT

I appreciate what I do and the effort
I put into it. I let go of the need to
have others do that for me.

I left home as early and as often as I could while growing up. It was not a pleasant place to be; not ever. I left every summer, and I spent most days working after-school jobs. One brother spent much more time at home and seemed to get a better start in life.

Shudda: You should have honored your parents more than you did.

Cudda: You could have done that if you hadn't been so selfish.

Wudda: If you had stayed longer and helped them more, you would have had more money to start out with and a better sense of what you wanted to do.

IMAWISE: Leaving home when you did was what you chose to do at the time to make yourself comfortable.

NEW THOUGHT

I accept my past actions as the best
I could do at the moment.

On a mountain road in New Mexico, I rounded a curve slowly and parked. It didn't seem to matter because a drunk driver met me head-on. He slid on the spring ice and skidded into the passenger side of my car. I left there feeling that I could have moved my car into the shoulder of the road, and that would have made a difference.

Shudda: That's why we have rules of the road. What were you doing on that mountain road, anyway?

Cudda: There's too much danger in climbing mountain roads in the spring; too much ice left.

Wudda: Sue the guy! It's his fault!

IMAWISE: What did you learn from this experience? You can ask yourself that at any time and gain insight from it.

NEW THOUGHT

I can take stock of any situation
I am in and learn from it.

I left the world of my parents to go into the world of my first husband. I hadn't learned to love myself at home, so I assumed that maybe I would feel better about myself being married. I didn't look long and far for that husband, either. I made a convenient choice and convinced him that marriage was the right thing for us to do.

Shudda: You must learn to take time to find the right partner, and the right one sees things the way you do.

Cudda: That marriage left a hopeless scar on you that is still there today.

Wudda: That husband was really unfair to you; he never saw your way or what you wanted out of life.

IMAWISE: You learned some powerful lessons about relationships from those years with this man. Cherish them.

NEW THOUGHT

The lessons I learn from all I do
are precious to me.

"Shop till you drop" was something I learned early. I had more legal ways to get the things I wanted than anyone I knew. I always felt most alive and most powerful when shopping. I now look back on all those years and find I had an addiction.

Shudda: The love of money and what we can do with it is always our undoing.

Cudda: You can't do anything about the past. There were so many reasons—good reasons—why you did what you did.

Wudda: All those credit card companies sending you pre-approved cards! Something needs to be done about them!

IMAWISE: There is no lesson so tough that you cannot learn it now. There is time to learn and a way to learn.

NEW THOUGHT

Compulsiveness often masks lessons
I need to learn. I can learn
one step at a time.

All of my cars have had hard lives. They have survived neglect, collisions and poor maintenance. I never took the time to learn what it takes to keep up a car.

Shudda: You will rue the day when your lack of care for your car costs you a bundle.

Cudda: What if your car explodes because you forgot to put oil in it?

Wudda: You were always so busy helping others that there just wasn't time to maintain your car.

IMAWISE: Whatever is given to you in this life is a loan. Nothing really belongs to anyone.

NEW THOUGHT

When I take good care of what is
given to me, I also take
good care of myself.

Things never go as I think they should. Prior to any event, I envision the event how I think it will go. After years of doing this, I finally figured out that my vision is a little bit off. I am still left with the feeling that I should have made better plans.

Shudda: If you fail to plan, you plan to fail.

Cudda: Ah, yes, and even the best laid plans will fail. Either way, it's hopeless.

Wudda: The dreams you have are just a bit out of reach. Aim lower, my dear.

IMAWISE: You can handle any situation. There is no real urgency to foresee events before they happen.

NEW THOUGHT

I enter new situations telling myself
that I can handle them. I enjoy
watching myself do that.

March 15

Just recently, I zeroed in on how helpful I had been to others over the years. I saw that I had really sacrificed some of the best years of my life to the causes of others—almost any cause, as a matter of fact. What I found in looking back was that I had abandoned my own cause. I now know that I needed to support my own cause.

Shudda: Hmmmm. *Others, Lord, yes others; let this my motto be.* . . .

Cudda: Now you are at midlife. What do you think you can do about this now? Stay the course, I say. Stay the course!

Wudda: You would have done it all differently if there had ever been anyone there for you. Too late—too impossible now!

IMAWISE: Being helpful to others can prompt you to do that for yourself now.

NEW THOUGHT

I can learn to give myself the kind
of care I offer to others.

I often say exactly what I think. I do not edit nor do I ease up on my opinions. I am especially good at this with loved ones who live with me. I leave many situations wishing that I had thought more before I spoke.

Shudda: Think before you speak! Think before you speak!

Cudda: That's like squirting too much toothpaste out of the tube. Now what can you do?

Wudda: Others around you have their faults, too. Can't you find their faults and spend more time dwelling on them?

IMAWISE: Mistakes with loved ones are common. Learn forgiveness and ways to make amends.

NEW THOUGHT

The mistakes I make are really teachers.
I make amends when I need
to make amends.

I have found it difficult to leave decisions that affect me in the hands of those who must make them. Many times I have left personal faith out of the situations that troubled me. I am learning about the place of personal faith in my life.

Shudda: Have you learned nothing about faith? Why, faith is everything!

Cudda: What about all the times that faith has worked for you? Did you just forget them?

Wudda: What would you do if God left you?

IMAWISE: Some of the hardest decisions require the most faith. It takes just a pinch of faith to get through them.

NEW THOUGHT

I can choose to use my faith to help
me at any time. I choose to watch
for evidence that it is working.

I wish I knew how to do more things, like paint with watercolors, skydive and write great fiction. I learned many things on my own as a way of surviving in childhood, but those things never seemed to be enough for me.

Shudda: You should know better than to suggest that others did not help you to learn the things that you wanted to learn. Be grateful!

Cudda: What if you leave this life with a lot of regrets because you didn't do the things that you wanted to do?

Wudda: It is unfair when others stand in the way of what you want to do in this life.

IMAWISE: You learned to do a great many things as a young person. At any point in your life now, you can do the same again.

NEW THOUGHT

I make choices that are in line with
what interests me. Those
choices are enough.

There were many things that I learned to do as a way to cope with a crazy family. These things helped me survive whatever was going on around me, and they got me out of the house. Some of those things are still interesting to me, and some fell by the wayside. I often think that I should have stayed with all of them.

Shudda: Where's your gratitude? If God gives you a talent, you must develop and use it to the fullest.

Cudda: Otherwise, God will come and take it away and give it to someone else. Then what?

Wudda: Do you think you really have time now to do all those things?

IMAWISE: You can choose if and when to develop the talents you have. You do not have to become a superstar to have used them well.

NEW THOUGHT

I use my talents as I see fit. I serve and I am blessed by my decisions.

Cats and dogs are my closest family. There was never any question in my mind about who was my next of kin. They were closer to me than the humans because they gave unconditional love. When my cat was very sick, I denied the seriousness of the problem. I now feel that I waited too long to seek a veterinarian's help.

Shudda: Now, don't you feel ashamed? How else would she get to the doctor? Shame! Shame!

Cudda: Things get worse when you don't pay attention to them. Don't you know that?

Wudda: So what you are saying is that you turned your back on your best friend in her time of need.

IMAWISE: Is it possible that you did the best you could at the moment with the understanding that you had?

NEW THOUGHT

I choose to make sense of the things I deny
in order to live in an honest way.

My first marriage saw me as the stepmother of two children. I saw them suffer from the nature of their biological parents' marriage and their lack of regular supervision. These two parents seemed to like fighting through their kids. When the situation became intolerable for me, I left and the kids were left to the ways of their parents.

Shudda: You should never have left those two kids, no matter how bad it got.

Cudda: You could have tried harder to help them understand what was going on.

Wudda: So you got help for yourself but left them, as it were, in a burning building?

IMAWISE: Those were tough times. You did what you could at the time. Sometimes you cannot save others.

NEW THOUGHT

There are times that I cannot save
others from their own fate.

Now I think long and hard before making any major decision. If I am stressed out, I am not likely to change my circumstances until I can see more clearly. It always takes a long time for me to realize this, though. I feel that I am now very slow in making most decisions.

Shudda: You should act more on faith and not so much on your own thoughts.

Cudda: I worry about whether you have the ability to make good decisions.

Wudda: Right. Coming from a crazy family, you probably don't have the right kind of background to make good decisions.

IMAWISE: You still have the ability to make good decisions. If you forget that, look back and count the good ones you've made.

NEW THOUGHT

I can recall the times I have acted
wisely in my own behalf.

March 23

When something hurts or angers me, I immediately go into denial. I act as if all is well and I am fine. If asked, I will respond, "I am fine." Then later, I will touch the hurt or anger within and find the wrong way to let go of it.

Shudda: Anger never pays. Crying when you are hurt only makes it worse.

Cudda: I'll tell you why you can't really handle your feelings. They don't lead to anything. They can't really help you.

Wudda: That's right. They only stir the crap and cause everyone around you to feel uncomfortable.

IMAWISE: Feelings are legitimate. They help you understand the boundaries you've set between yourself and others.

NEW THOUGHT

I choose to feel and honor my feelings.
From knowing my feelings,
I can learn my limits.

All the therapists I know say it is good to talk about your feelings. That may be true, but it doesn't make it any easier to do. I have long kept to myself all feelings, good or bad, because they felt overwhelming.

Shudda: Feelings are a lack of faith.

Cudda: You could have taught yourself more about them so that they wouldn't feel so scary.

Wudda: Feelings are impossible to change, so why try?

IMAWISE: Sharing feelings with a trusted person is a healthy way to manage them.

NEW THOUGHT

I can share my feelings, good or bad,
as a way to manage them.

I often wish I had received more help for my problems as a child. It wasn't available at home and in fact, it was much safer to stifle my feelings than to let them show. Family members stomped on a feeling if they saw it coming. I wish I had found someone to talk to about all that I stifled.

Shudda: No point in looking into that now. Just think pleasant thoughts!

Cudda: It's hopeless to look back. What can you do now?

Wudda: If others couldn't help you then, they probably can't help now, so what's the point?

IMAWISE: Stifling your feelings was all you knew to do. It helped you to cope. Now you have better choices.

NEW THOUGHT

I choose today to deal with
the feelings I have.

I do not know the meaning of the word "patient." I have been told I need more patience. Some have offered to pray that I would develop more patience. Though I see the need, I begged off, sure that I would not like situations that help "develop patience."

Shudda: Patient is as patient does. You must learn to wait.

Cudda: If you have to wait for something, might as well spend that time thinking about all the possible outcomes.

Wudda: If others make you wait, then that is their fault. You can't change them—it's impossible.

IMAWISE: You can be as patient as you want to be. Waiting can be filled with wonderful discovery.

NEW THOUGHT

If my situation tells me to wait, I can
use the time in a good way.

March 27

I've often found that I compare myself with others, no matter what situation I am in. Somehow, their life is better, fuller, richer. Their way is the way I should travel, I think. I do not see their problems; I just assume they have fewer than I do. I assume that their path is better and easier than mine.

Shudda: Others who have it easier are living by faith. If you want to be God-like, you live by faith.

Cudda: You will find that another's way is probably better than the one you travel.

Wudda: I think you must travel alone, if the trip is worth anything at all to you.

IMAWISE: Your path is carved and cared for by you. If you think it needs to be better, make it so.

NEW THOUGHT

I improve my path when
I see the need.

Why didn't I realize my dreams sooner? I could have been working on them for the last 20 years, while I was doing this other thing over here. I lost a lot of valuable time. Look at where I could be if I had only started sooner.

Shudda: If you had done things in the proper way early on, you wouldn't be behind now.

Cudda: The reason you couldn't do it is because your family never supported you.

Wudda: Your hopes and dreams from that time are out of reach, even if you wanted to reach them now.

IMAWISE: You can make choices now to support the dreams you have.

NEW THOUGHT

I choose each moment to support my dreams, in thought, word and actions, regardless of my circumstances.

March 29

I have heard so many thousands of reasons why I can't do what I want to do with my life that I quit talking about my hopes and dreams. It felt unsafe to discuss them with just anybody. Others spent much time telling me why my dreams were too tough to work on and too impossible to come true.

Shudda: There are good reasons for the truth that others share, especially if they are your elders.

Cudda: What if you tried to live your dreams and you failed?

Wudda: You would take a lot of crap from those same people who told you not to pursue your dreams, that's what!

IMAWISE: Your dreams are worth striving for, and failure is just a single lesson on the way to success.

NEW THOUGHT

My dreams enliven me and awaken
me to my potential.

It has been a real strain all these years to get the approval of others. It seemed necessary—a real effort that bent me over and back again. I must have looked like a pretzel. I simply got tired of it. A friend pointed out that getting approval from some people could be the worst of all outcomes. For instance, if both Hitler and Billy Graham approved of my actions, then what would that say about my actions?

Shudda: It is very important to do things so that you are well-liked. Be ladylike at all times.

Cudda: If you don't, what will people think? What will they say?

Wudda: They will accuse you of not understanding their point of view, and then you will look stupid.

IMAWISE: Seek your own approval. Know what pleases you. That is enough.

NEW THOUGHT

I look inward for the approval I need.

I long to take matters into my own hands and settle some of my issues in a childish way. I often daydream about "teaching others a lesson." I do not really get to do this, except in my own thoughts.

Shudda: These kinds of thoughts get you in big trouble! Don't even think them!

Cudda: Thinking this way is just asking for the worst to happen. Look out!

Wudda: Just thinking will get you into the worst trouble of all. Others can sense what you are thinking.

IMAWISE: Thinking about revenge is very human. It can take away the potential of acting it out.

NEW THOUGHT

Good and bad thoughts are human. I can use either to help me determine my plan of action.

APRIL

Excuses are only
useful to help explain
why I didn't do what
was important to me to
do. They never help
me reach a goal.

April 1

This was the first day of my first marriage. We sneaked off to tie the knot in a civil ceremony. Looking back now, this might have been a great clue. Later the choice turned to divorce. I learned the importance of starting out on the right foot.

Shudda: You ran off and left others out of this important day.

Cudda: You could have let family in on it because when you leave them out, you can expect the worst.

Wudda: The reason this was not a good idea is that it was not open and honest with everyone who is important in your life.

IMAWISE: Love is a great force and a great teacher. This marriage and its collapse led to many great lessons.

NEW THOUGHT

Regrets lead me to think I might have
done better. Lessons come wrapped
in odd packages.

In looking back, I recall never having much patience for the oldest people in my life. A high-energy person, it was very hard for me to slow down to the pace of the elderly. As a teenager, I often frustrated my grandmother with my angry outbursts. I did not understand the source of this anger.

Shudda: You could've given her a heart attack.

Cudda: What if in the middle of your anger she dropped dead?

Wudda: Think how unfair you were to someone who was just trying to help you. How can you live with yourself now?

IMAWISE: Much of your anger came from things you did not understand and could not change. Forgiveness is in order.

NEW THOUGHT

I am no longer captive of my past mistakes.
I choose forgiveness.

When I first saw my inner child in a dream, I was amazed at how distant I felt from her. I could see that she looked like me. I could hear her and she sounded like me. It seemed I could feel how she felt right away. I often quit listening for that reason.

Shudda: It's just like you to walk away from a needy person. Shame! Shame!

Cudda: Think of what you could have done and become if you only had chosen to listen to her. . . .

Wudda: You probably told her that it was impossible for you to listen to her.

IMAWISE: Listening to your inner child is listening to a starved spirit. She is hard to understand at times. Keep trying.

NEW THOUGHT

I do not have to do everything perfectly
all at once. Instead, I can take
my time and learn.

There were many adventures offered to me as I entered adulthood. One of them was a trip to Belize with a friend I had met on the island of Bonaire. There I learned to scuba dive and found immense treasures of unmatched beauty on the ocean floor.

Shudda: Scuba diving is very dangerous and you hardly know how to do it.

Cudda: You could have been killed, do you know that?

Wudda: In foreign countries they really like to jail Americans for little or no reason.

IMAWISE: Adventure of any kind is just another lesson, presenting its own challenges.

NEW THOUGHT

I learn about myself and the world
around me from the adventures
I give myself.

April 5

Long ago, I wanted to write, and the only way I knew to get started was to start writing about something I knew. I talked about writing with close friends and found most of them pretty skeptical. After each discussion I found that my own thoughts were telling me that this was an impossible dream.

Shudda: There is a proper way to start anything. You need to go to school.

Cudda: See, your thoughts told you why it is so hard to do.

Wudda: If you try it and fail, you will remember these warnings.

IMAWISE: Trying something and failing is admirable. Following your dreams may lead to the most pleasant parts of life.

NEW THOUGHT

Trying, failing and succeeding all teach
me things I need to know.

One constant regret I have about the first 42 years of living are my choices in the foods that I have eaten. I live in a place where vegetables are hard to come by and are quite expensive. Even as a child, I found that I ate all the bad things and ate in a pattern that led to an eating disorder.

Shudda: You are what you eat, missy!

Cudda: What if all these years you had eaten your vegetables and drunk eight glasses of water a day?

Wudda: Your skin would glow and you would be healthier than you are today.

IMAWISE: Some early choices in food were out of your hands. You can choose to take better care of yourself today.

NEW THOUGHT

How I care for my body and my choices
in foods are up to me each day.

April 7

When circumstances became uncomfortable at a previous work site, I found myself ready to quit. I never felt I was a quitter, but I found the way we served clients to be intolerable. Some kids were treated better than others. Who received better treatment was determined by my superiors, and it seemed to be based on race. I kept thinking there was something I could do to change this.

Shudda: Giving up never helped anybody.

Cudda: If you had tried harder to get everyone to change, you would know now what you can really do.

Wudda: This was the fault of someone else, who used you to take the blame.

IMAWISE: Your actions spoke of your commitment to fairness toward all the kids involved here.

NEW THOUGHT

I support my own principles fully
with my actions.

I still think I could have been more persuasive in a number of work situations where I witnessed clients and counselors acting inappropriately with each other. I stated my case in a professional manner and found that everyone seemed puzzled by my comments.

Shudda: Now, see: this is what happens when you speak and stand all alone. Feel like a fool yet?

Cudda: This was hopeless; you couldn't do anything because you were not in charge.

Wudda: You could not change this because you didn't find the right way to say what you needed to say.

IMAWISE: It is wise to remember that some folks choose not to hear the very things they need to hear.

NEW THOUGHT

I say what I need to say and leave the choice to hear it up to others.

April 9

For years I have lived a co-dependent life, basing all my decisions on what others do and think. Gaining the approval of others was a top priority of mine. I always looked outward for someone else to find my answer. I took parts of others' personalities and slapped them onto my own in the hope of making myself interesting enough to others. I left my natural self buried under all this rubble.

Shudda: When God gives you gifts, you do not, and I repeat, *do not* bury them.

Cudda: Right. You could have learned to use them. What if you had just tried a little harder?

Wudda: This is something you could have tried on your own.

IMAWISE: In a dysfunctional family, co-dependency was a means of survival. Today, you can choose another way.

NEW THOUGHT

I try various ways of relating to others today.
I learn from mistakes and move on.

I stayed up too late last night and slept very poorly as a result. Morning came all too soon and the routine of the new day took me on before I was ready.

Shudda: Now there's an important issue. You just have to get enough sleep the night before to do anything the next day.

Cudda: You could have started earlier the day before and then you could have gone to bed early enough, eh?

Wudda: What's really unfair is the number of things you have to do here at the house. See what the family makes you do?

IMAWISE: Have you noticed that you learn from whatever situation you are in? Have you noticed that the learning feels good?

NEW THOUGHT

I learn what I need most in whatever situation I am in.

April 11

Long lunches are a rarity for me. One day I took one and missed three important phone calls, one of which asked me where I was. Inside, I felt like a disobedient child. For a moment, I forgot my professional nature and began to line up excuses for the boss.

Shudda: There are rules about these things for a good reason.

Cudda: What if the boss got the idea that you did this all the time?

Wudda: It would be hard for him to accept that you did anything else, eh?

IMAWISE: Taking a break for whatever reason is often a good thing. You know when you need to do that.

NEW THOUGHT

I take time out when I need it.
I refuse to become defensive
about my own needs.

When I can't see my way through a situation and am totally frustrated with it, I find peace in prayer. It is not the first thing I think about doing. It is often the last.

Shudda: Prayer changes things. You ought to know that. What would God say to you about refusing to pray?

Cudda: You always have an excuse for why you don't pray. How do you think that sounds to the Almighty?

Wudda: I'm sure you would have prayed sooner if your parents had taught you to do that more often.

IMAWISE: Prayer is the key and you think about it when it has the most potential to help you.

NEW THOUGHT

I choose prayer when I am ready
to receive its benefits.

In the last 42 years, I have found one great medicine that can be used in most situations—even the worst ones. That medicine is laughter. I found what was funny in growing up at home and still today find humor in the absurd.

Shudda: You should not laugh at others. That embarrasses them. Shame! Shame!

Cudda: Right, and then you look silly. What if they laughed at you?

Wudda: What else can you do with the crap others fire at you?

IMAWISE: Laughter is a great medicine and a great way to cope. It has saved you many times.

NEW THOUGHT

When I find humor in the situations I face,
I can cope with just about anything.

Everyone around me is always trying to find the "right" mate. It is as if people can't last much longer without one. I got caught up in the search as well and spent years looking for my "soulmate." I never found this person and ended up frustrated.

Shudda: All in God's timing. You will find the right person when God is ready for you to find him.

Cudda: I think you have reason to be worried. Look how old you are!

Wudda: I'd start looking everywhere because you only have a little time left.

IMAWISE: I would like to see you learn to be very comfortable with yourself and then take the person you are into a relationship.

NEW THOUGHT

I can learn to be comfortable and loving
toward myself. I can then choose to
be in a relationship or not.

109

I pushed myself to finish graduate school in record time. I worked double time to make that happen. It did happen, and I ignored all the feelings I had about my divorce in order to do it. When I finished, I looked around me and asked my teachers, "Now what?"

Shudda: Hurry never helped anybody. Rush, rush, rush to what?

Cudda: You can't do good work in a rush.

Wudda: Rushing can ruin even the best hopes and dreams, not to mention your health.

IMAWISE: This was a rush job and it led you to understand the real pace you need to set for yourself.

NEW THOUGHT

I can choose the pace that
fits my highest good.

I've lived in several states, and I find each community fascinating. I wonder if the people there love or dislike the place where they live and what their lifestyles are like. I visit many places and always imagine living wherever I visit. Many times when moving, I've wondered if I left too soon.

Shudda: Can't you stay put? What do you think that moving around so much says to people who might hire you?

Cudda: It says you are not stable; not stable at all!

Wudda: Each time you move, you are less likely to find the help you need in the new community. Just stay to yourself!

IMAWISE: Moving offers many opportunities to learn how to adjust.

NEW THOUGHT

I can adjust to a new place when
I see the need to move.

April 17

Push! Push! No patience at all. Keep moving. Keep going on. Don't stop! This is what I have said to myself for years. I convinced myself that I did not need rest, that there was so much to do to help others, and that rest would come only at the point of exhaustion.

Shudda: Service to others—that's where real life lies. Serve! Serve! Serve!

Cudda: Keep trying and you will get it—helping others is the only way to feel good about yourself.

Wudda: Your hopes and dreams are tied up in helping others, and the only way you will feel satisfied is to see the smiling faces of others who need you.

IMAWISE: The body—any body, your body—has limits. It is a gift to you and you can choose to use it wisely.

NEW THOUGHT

What I do with my body is completely up to me. I choose to treat it with respect.

I often become aware of injustice long before those around me are willing to acknowledge it. Others know it just as I know it, but they choose to be silent. I find I can't keep quiet.

Shudda: There you go again, starting trouble. What makes you think you are right this time?

Cudda: This is hopeless! You haven't enough trouble yet, have you?

Wudda: I'll tell you, little girl, no one's going to help you through this one. You'll be standing alone.

IMAWISE: Recognizing injustice and doing something about it are choices that lead to learning how to make things better.

NEW THOUGHT

When I choose to address injustice I accept the consequences of my actions.

I like to learn how to do many new things. I find I approach most things with an open mind about how well I will do them. When I do this, I usually uncover a new talent. It makes me wish I had appreciated the talents I knew I had much earlier than I did.

Shudda: Do not bury your talents under a bushel basket. You must use them for the good of others.

Cudda: What if you had paid attention to what you have been given and used it well?

Wudda: Your parents only supported the talents that they liked in you, so how could you be any different?

IMAWISE: Talent is a process of discovery, and what you do with each new discovery is up to you.

NEW THOUGHT

I study ways I want to use my talents.

I have some talents, such as singing, that I rarely use anymore. I still love to sing, and yet I have put it on the back burner for a while. I long to find a place where my singing will be appreciated again. I just haven't chosen to use this talent.

Shudda: If you don't use it, you will lose it. God doesn't give gifts so that they will be shoved aside.

Cudda: Think of others who do not have this ability. You need to spend more time using what you have been given.

Wudda: There's a dream out the window. How many more do you think you will let fly away?

IMAWISE: The gifts we have are to be used at different times. You do not have to be all things to all people.

NEW THOUGHT

I can use my gifts as I see fit. My job is to be the best steward of what I have been given.

I always worry about what I eat. I find that I usually eat too fast and too much. When I get hungry I worry about what to eat. I recently discovered that I know very little about planning and preparing good meals.

Shudda: You are what you eat! This is not new information!

Cudda: You could take the time to read and apply the information on nutrition that is available. What are you waiting for?

Wudda: Changing your eating habits is an impossible task for someone as busy as you.

IMAWISE: Your body is a temple, given over to your care. The decisions you make affect the condition of your temple.

NEW THOUGHT

My body deserves the best
care I can give it.

When there's a job to do, I look far beyond my own part to see how the other parts of the job are interconnected. I observe others doing their jobs. This often leads me to worry about how others do their job, whether they will do them, etc.

Shudda: Someone has to be sure that things get done in the right way.

Cudda: Usually no one else is looking out for all the parts, so stay with it!

Wudda: You could just do the job alone and get it done quicker and better.

IMAWISE: You can choose to pay attention to your part and *learn* to let others do theirs.

NEW THOUGHT

I am not in charge of all the parts of anything.
I can do my part and get great
satisfaction from it.

April 23

Worrying about how others will do their part has led me to be co-dependent in anything I do. I spend time figuring out what I consider is the best way to do anything. The best way is always the way I figure out. I then think that I must "sell" that to others.

Shudda: Look, somebody's gotta do it. Might as well be you.

Cudda: If you don't, who will?

Wudda: If you do it, it will get taken care of, right?

IMAWISE: You do not have to work that hard. There are many good ways to do most things.

NEW THOUGHT

I can let go of trying to be the best.
I can learn from watching
how others do things.

I still find that I worry quite a bit, even when others are doing their parts. I wonder when they will finish, how well they will do their jobs and if I can count on them. This includes everything from chores at home to work in the office and studio.

Shudda: As I have said many times, there's a proper way to do things and you know what that is.

Cudda: What if you stand on the sidelines and say nothing and the project turns out terrible?

Wudda: It is unfair to you if others don't do their jobs up to snuff and you have to take the blame.

IMAWISE: You are responsible only for your part. Letting go of the other parts will free up time for other things you want to do.

NEW THOUGHT

I take charge of my own role
in any work that I do.

My first marriage failed. It led me to the obvious conclusion that I should have never married at all. I saw marriage as a waste of my time. When I look at the lessons I learned from my first partner, I could let go of some of the guilt.

Shudda: I still think you should have stayed and tried to make it work. Divorce is a blight on you and your family.

Cudda: Yes; there were many things that you did not try, and one of them was probably the answer.

Wudda: Or you are probably one of those people who need to be alone and really can't live with anyone.

IMAWISE: Failure is not disaster; it is a group of tough lessons that you are choosing to learn. Stay with it.

NEW THOUGHT

I learn about strength from
tough situations.

Low on cash, with no job and in need of a vacation, I took what I had and headed for the island of Bonaire in the Caribbean. I learned to scuba dive there and saw the most incredible sights I have seen on Earth.

Shudda: Now, how are you going to eat? Squandered your cash again, did you?

Cudda: You could have gone to work right away instead and put off this trip.

Wudda: What would your parents have said about spending money on a trip, when you have responsibilities here at home? And what about your retirement plans?

IMAWISE: Guilt blocks lessons that could be learned about rest, recovery and the need to provide for yourself.

NEW THOUGHT

I practice letting go of guilt I feel
over decisions I make.

Out of work and late in the year to be seeking a position in my field, it dawned on me that I needed a job. I panicked, thinking I would not find work to support myself. This led me to believe that I would suffer greatly and could end up out on the streets as a bag lady.

Shudda: That's exactly what will happen to you, unless you find a steady job that has benefits and long-term security.

Cudda: You need to find your place in the work world and stay put.

Wudda: Right! If you don't, what do you think will happen? How in the world will you take care of yourself?

IMAWISE: There are many honorable ways to earn a living. God has given you desires that can make that happen at any point in your life.

NEW THOUGHT

I am capable of supporting myself
in ways that please me.

Over the years I've felt that I rarely fit in anywhere that I have worked. I try very hard to fit in and end up giving too much of myself. In the long run, I suffer and find others at fault because I believe that I should fit in at most places.

Shudda: You can fit in if you want to fit in. Just watch how others do it so you can feel comfortable.

Cudda: You just have to try much harder.

Wudda: Your parents would be appalled at how you have given up so easily.

IMAWISE: "Fitting in" is not always what you need to do. You may decide to create a situation that fits you, instead of waiting for others to create it for you.

NEW THOUGHT

I create and live in an environment that fits me.
I do this with each decision I make.

As a step-parent, I hardly knew the proper role to have with my two kids. I worried constantly about interfering with their interests, and I was not sure how to support these interests.

Shudda: Children need guidance about what interests them. You should have given them this.

Cudda: What if they were left alone to just come up with their own interests? Don't you think that could be dangerous?

Wudda: What would your mother say? Children need to be guided in their choice of dreams.

IMAWISE: Children come with a natural capacity to unlock their own dreams. You can be a companion on their journey and offer needed help without interfering.

NEW THOUGHT

I do not have to take charge of another
person's journey. I can be a helper
and assist when needed.

Decisions take me a long time to reach. I worry over them, spend much time analyzing all possible solutions, everyone's reactions to my choices, and what is best in the short and long runs. I spend so much time on decision-making that I rob myself of fun and play and drive others crazy in the meantime.

Shudda: Decisions actually take more time than you give them.

Cudda: The worst results are the ones that can't be seen from where you are, so you need to take a lot of time.

Wudda: It is impossible to make decisions quickly and then live with the outcome.

IMAWISE: Take the time you need to make any decision you face. There is no set pace that is right for everyone.

NEW THOUGHT

I choose my pace for
making decisions.

MAY

So, who chose the
direction in which
I am heading?

May 1

Each spring the new clothing on the market thrills me. I usually want to buy everything I see. After much thought, I narrow it down to a few things. But I find that I'm still wanting—always wanting more than I can afford or that will fit me.

Shudda: The love of *things* is like the love of money. It is the root of all evil.

Cudda: You "needed" those new things to stay up with fashion and keep the "right" look.

Wudda: You had all those dreams of traveling and there it all went—poof! Gone in the clothes budget!

IMAWISE: What is it that attracts you about these new lines of clothing? If you can get to the bottom of that, it will be a clue for your own journey.

NEW THOUGHT

My attraction to new things helps me
understand some work I need to
do on my own issues.

In the early years, there were just two of us, my brother and me. He always seemed bent on raining on my parade. I kept anything that was precious close to me so that he could not find it. I also kept everything of mine safely out of his reach so that no harm could come to any of it.

Shudda: What kind of sister were you, anyway? You should have tried to trust your own brother.

Cudda: What if everyone had treated you that way? Aren't you exaggerating?

Wudda: He would have done anything he wanted because your mom and dad did not discipline anyone.

IMAWISE: Protecting your own things is natural. We all do it. It was difficult to trust when you felt everything had to be guarded.

NEW THOUGHT

Learning to trust may be a slow process.
I will give myself the time I need.

I always felt the need to keep my personal travel plans from my family. This came after announcing a wonderful trip to southeast Asia. My mother told me that people of a different color than her family were very violent. When I contested her assumption, she restated her opinion, insisting that I was in real danger.

Shudda: What's a mother to do? When you are a mom, you will understand.

Cudda: She said that because . . . well, what else was she going to say?

Wudda: Exactly. You didn't even think of inviting her.

IMAWISE: The level of trust your mother had for other people does not have to be your level of trust.

NEW THOUGHT

I learn to trust based on my own experiences
with others and not on someone
else's opinion of them.

I celebrate life all year long, and birthdays are an important time. I have learned to celebrate birthdays anytime of the year that it strikes me to do so. I still remember a birthday, and I let a person's life speak to me about ways to celebrate with him or her throughout the year.

Shudda: You should always remember someone's birthday. How would you feel if yours was forgotten?

Cudda: If you forget someone's birthday, you're headed for their disappointment.

Wudda: No one is going to be there to remind you of this kind of thing. You will have to do it on your own.

IMAWISE: There are many ways to celebrate the lives of those important to you.

NEW THOUGHT

I find wonderful reasons to celebrate
the lives of those closest to me
—all year long.

As a child, play was the last thing on my mind. Play came rarely in a dysfunctional family life. So as an adult, I look for unusual ways to play. Still, the hard part is to set aside the time to play and then actually do it.

Shudda: There is a time to play and a time to be serious.

Cudda: The reason you couldn't play as much as you wanted to as a child is that your parents thought it wasn't good for you.

Wudda: Sometimes it is just too difficult to find time to play . . . and how important is it, anyway?

IMAWISE: No matter how old you are, play is vital to your good health the way that laughter is.

NEW THOUGHT

Play and work are equally
important in my life.

Even playing with my stepchildren was something hard for me to do. They always wanted me to join whatever they were doing. I wanted to join them. Yet I felt there were more important things, even crucial things, that had to be done. I often felt that I did not play enough with them.

Shudda: There are many more important things than play. Children have to learn that by example.

Cudda: What else could you do? There was so much work to be done in that house.

Wudda: It is impossible to be with the kids every single time they feel they need you.

IMAWISE: The choices you made in the past about play can teach you now about what is important for your health.

NEW THOUGHT

I set aside much time for play and join
in with others when it fits
with my needs.

133

I remember feeling guilty anytime someone did something nice for me. I felt that I owed them something right away, or that they had an agenda behind the kind act. I never could quite accept that nice things do happen, even to me.

Shudda: Nice things do happen, but you have to make them happen.

Cudda: Watch out! Nice things usually come with a price.

Wudda: And the price is usually sky-high!

IMAWISE: Nice things happen to everyone from time to time. It is a gift of the universe, not always the product of a hidden agenda.

NEW THOUGHT

I can accept nice things that happen to me.
I allow myself to enjoy them.

Compliments were hard to accept, too. Why did others see good in me, enough to comment on it? What do you do with a compliment? What is behind it?

Shudda: There's always something behind it. You have to watch for what they really want.

Cudda: Yes, it's there and you can't see it. Just watch out!

Wudda: You can't see what they want because they hide it under the compliment, waiting for you to bite. Get it?

IMAWISE: Many of us find compliments hard to accept. There is nothing more to do than to say "Thank you."

NEW THOUGHT

I accept graciously
the compliments I receive.

I believe that others trust more than I do. I usually operated with a low trust level and to this day struggle with the issue of trust. I either trust too much or too little. Either way I find trouble. With my partner I find that I often trust too little.

Shudda: Trust is the key and it comes to you from above.

Cudda: If you worked harder at it, it could come easier.

Wudda: You and you alone have to learn to trust. No one can do it for you.

IMAWISE: This is a tough one for you, but you can do it one step at a time. Accept where you are with the issue of trust today.

NEW THOUGHT

I accept that trust is hard for me and
I give myself all the time I need
to learn to trust more.

Fear has been a constant and lifelong companion. As a little person, I learned that there was a lot to fear. Fear paralyzed me and kept me from doing things that interested me. It kept me from exploring what appealed to me.

Shudda: Fear is the absence of faith. God does not appreciate that!

Cudda: If you are filled with fear, you will draw the worst situations and people to you.

Wudda: You are being unfair to your Creator when you set aside your faith and live in fear instead.

IMAWISE: Fear is a signal that something you cherish is in danger. This signal is still important because it helps define your limits and shows when to use your faith.

NEW THOUGHT

Fear is a new kind of teacher, showing me my
limits in any situation. It also helps
me see when to use my faith.

May 11

I can't remember much about my child-hood dreams—that is, what I wanted to be when I grew up. I am sure that I wanted to please my parents as a way to get a chunk of their attention. If I had hopes and dreams of my own, I know I gave them up for something more impressive to the family.

Shudda: It is important to honor your parents with what you do.

Cudda: You can honor the whole family with your choice of profession.

Wudda: You have to figure this one out on your own. No one can do it for you.

IMAWISE: If you gave up a dream that you still want, it can be yours. You can give it to yourself.

NEW THOUGHT

What are my dreams today? What am I doing to make them come true?

My sex life has worried me over the years. Not that it was wild and crazy, but it wasn't what I thought it should be. I did not know what to do differently, but I had this nagging feeling that it was not all I could make it. I am learning how to be healthier in this area.

Shudda: We will *not* discuss this now or at anytime. Such things are personal!

Cudda: There was not much time to learn about these things and really, what could you do?

Wudda: No one can tell you about this; you have to learn it on your own.

IMAWISE: Sexual activity is a form of communication. Like any other form of communicating, you can improve it.

NEW THOUGHT

I can improve any form of
communication I use.

An argument broke the stillness of the new day. Arguments indicate that a relationship is about to end or get dangerous. I often push people too hard for something to happen. I know I need to leave them alone to do what they need to do.

Shudda: Arguments mean that you are just being your usual difficult self.

Cudda: If you ask me, arguments get out of control far too often, and people leave each other too quickly.

Wudda: If others leave you, that is their fault, and there is nothing you can do about it.

IMAWISE: Arguments raise the intensity of a relationship from time to time. They have the power to clear the air and set realistic limits for partners.

NEW THOUGHT

I use arguments to clarify my
position, clear the air and
set reasonable limits.

The men in my life have found that if they wait long enough to do their household chores, I will do them. I love a clean house. I get angry when I end up doing someone's work for them, and I do not blame myself. I usually blame them for my choice to do their work.

Shudda: What's wrong with doing their work? They are tired and it *has* to be done.

Cudda: If you wait too long, the house will be filthy and someone will think it's your fault.

Wudda: If others don't do their share, you are justified in giving them a hard time. It's not fair to you.

IMAWISE: You can do your share and let the rest go. If others do not care to do theirs, they may face the consequences.

NEW THOUGHT

I let others face the consequences
of their actions.

May 15

When I headed for Mexico for a needed vacation and some scuba diving, a hurricane hit the very city I chose to visit. There was a great deal of devastation to the entire area. Tourism stopped. The cleanup began. I chose not to visit because I would have worked my entire vacation.

Shudda: You have everything you need in life and more. Why couldn't you help those less fortunate than you?

Cudda: What is the worst that could happen to you if you helped out?

Wudda: You have the skills they really needed.

IMAWISE: Sounds like you needed a break from work. Taking a break is a healthy thing to do.

NEW THOUGHT

I rest from work when I need to.
I take rest as seriously
as I do work.

142

There were a number of difficult situations I faced when I should have left well-enough alone. I should have stood by and let others learn whatever they could. Instead, I often interfered to show them *what* to learn and *how* to learn it.

Shudda: Now see here, someone's got to show people the right things to learn or they won't learn what is important.

Cudda: What if everyone jumped ship like you are suggesting and there was no one left to pass on needed information?

Wudda: It is not your fault if they don't understand that you are trying to help them.

IMAWISE: There are times to step in and times to step out and let others learn by themselves. You learn the difference by doing.

NEW THOUGHT

I learn when to step in and when to
step back. Each lesson is
just that: a lesson.

May 17

I watched others get hurt by people who held extreme and unfounded biases against them. Often I jumped in and stated my beliefs about this unfair behavior.

Shudda: It is not your job to decide who is right and who is wrong.

Cudda: It is hopeless to try to change prejudice. Look at how many other people have tried and failed. Some of them are dead.

Wudda: It is impossible to help others free themselves. What makes you think you are able to do such a thing?

IMAWISE: Standing up for unfair treatment often means some folks won't like you or what you say.

NEW THOUGHT

I choose right action based on
principles important to me.

In any given crowd, I will be the one to ask questions. I look around and it seems that everyone is understanding what is going on. I am often the one who challenges what is being done or said, much to the annoyance of others. I am often the one who doesn't understand.

Shudda: There's something to be said for keeping yourself quiet and accepting. You do not have to challenge everything.

Cudda: Nothing could ever get finished if everyone spoke up like you do.

Wudda: If you have to speak up, it would help if you would find something right with the group.

IMAWISE: Asking questions is the way you learn. If others find this irritating, that is their problem.

NEW THOUGHT

I have the right to question what
goes on around me.

Low on the trust level all my life, I find that trust is my toughest issue. Some of the people I know are worthy of trust, and clearly others are not. I find it difficult at times to tell the difference.

Shudda: If we trust God, we know when to trust.

Cudda: You could trust if you could just let go.

Wudda: You can blame others if they make it hard on you—like your parents did.

IMAWISE: Trust is something you learn and build. You cannot accomplish this overnight.

NEW THOUGHT

I am learning about trust
each day I live.

Sunday is usually a family day in our house. We take rides in the country or mountains, eat out and generally spend the day together. I enjoy it but still feel pulled to do things for my career or for the house. I rarely find a solution for this that I can live with.

Shudda: A woman's work is never done. You need to please others before you please yourself.

Cudda: If you don't put others first, then what would it be like for you if your loved ones suddenly were not around anymore?

Wudda: If there's too much to do, you just haven't organized well enough, now have you?

IMAWISE: There are many pleasing ways to use your time. Your choices reflect your most pressing need at the moment.

NEW THOUGHT

The tension I feel about which
activities to choose means that I am
an important part of many things.

I fear becoming too happy or content. Somewhere along the way, I learned that if I felt too happy, I would lose whatever helped me feel that way.

Shudda: It is a good thing not to get too happy. You make silly decisions from that viewpoint.

Cudda: I can tell you why you must not get too happy. It is because God rains on your parade when you are too happy.

Wudda: If you get too happy, someone will take away that happiness and you will be all alone.

IMAWISE: Feelings come and go—that is normal. You can be happy or sad and live through both.

NEW THOUGHT

I can manage my feelings
—happy or sad.

When I left my family home, I immediately felt that I was not ready to live on my own. I felt ill-prepared to deal with life. I had a nagging feeling that I should have left home much later than I did.

Shudda: You should be thankful for the start that your parents gave you.

Cudda: You just needed an excuse for someone else to pay the bills a little while longer. Do you have any idea how much meat costs?

Wudda: You can only get so much help. You have to do this alone.

IMAWISE: You left when you did because it was the only thing you could do at the time. You learned the lessons that followed very well.

NEW THOUGHT

Hindsight on my decisions leads me to
conclusions that I have done the
best I could each time.

I made the decision to discuss my grand-mother's death with her long before her time actually came. It was much easier than I imagined. Other family members seemed put off by this when they heard about it.

Shudda: Death is a private matter, not to be discussed.

Cudda: What if everyone in the family had done this?

Wudda: It was unfair for them to get upset with you. Why wouldn't you ask older members of the family first?

IMAWISE: Your relationship with your grandmother included her impending death. You and she needed to feel all right with that upcoming event.

NEW THOUGHT

When something is important,
I face it by talking it over.

Like many other women I know, I collect things: clothes, accessories, jewelry. Only when it comes time to clean do I realize how much stuff has accumulated in my home. I should give more of it away to others who could use it.

Shudda: You should be thankful for the things you have or you may lose them.

Cudda: That's right. A fire could take them all away.

Wudda: And what would you do then? You would have only yourself to blame.

IMAWISE: You are thankful for what you have and you *are* generous.

NEW THOUGHT

Having the things I need and want does
not lead to their destruction.
I am grateful daily.

In my travels here and abroad, extreme need jumps out at me. I am touched by people who must rise above severe poverty in order to live and love. I often feel that I should do more to help others in need.

Shudda: That's it. See, we can never do enough for others. They are waiting for your help, all of them.

Cudda: What if you were in their position? How would you feel?

Wudda: How long do you think they can wait for help? What will happen if they do not get it?

IMAWISE: God gives each of us a measure of talent aimed at times and ways we can help. We do not have to be all things to all people.

NEW THOUGHT

I do not want to be all things
to all people.

I am acutely aware of clothing that is fashionable and have spent years keeping up with the trends. Still, no matter where I go I look outward to see who is dressed best. I am rarely satisfied with my own attire.

Shudda: Appearance does not count. You are what you eat and you can't cover that up.

Cudda: It will cost you too much to keep up with others. Why don't you make a new outfit every night?

Wudda: You spend too much on clothes as it is. Don't you feel guilty about that?

IMAWISE: I would like you to be pleased with your appearance. Honor who you are on the inside and outside in all the situations you face.

NEW THOUGHT

I think about myself in a way that leaves
me content with who I am
and how I look.

Working hard for 20 years as a counselor, I've abandoned myself at times. During those times I forget that I am a normal human being with real needs. I attend to my own crises, but not to the normal human needs for breaks, time off and basic things.

Shudda: Idle hands are the devil's workshop. Busy is happy.

Cudda: There is so much to do that it is next to impossible to take regular breaks and time off.

Wudda: If you just keep your nose to the grindstone, you will make the grade.

IMAWISE: You have real needs. You know this. Take care of them.

NEW THOUGHT

When I find that I need something, I meet that need in a reasonable time frame.

I have difficulty tending to my own medical needs. It seems I wait until I have no choice but to go see a doctor. I will deny the pain or discomfort as long as I can.

Shudda: Doctors may help you heal, but all they want is your money. You have to watch them.

Cudda: What if you let an ailment go too long and it progresses to a dangerous level?

Wudda: Your hopes and dreams would go out the window, that's what.

IMAWISE: Taking good care of yourself means seeing a doctor regularly. Good health is a choice.

NEW THOUGHT

I choose habits that support
good health.

Sometimes I wish I had spent more time attending school. I would have completed my studies at a younger age and have more energy now for projects that are important to me. I look back on years spent outside of learning situations and sometimes see wasted time.

Shudda: We are always learning, so what difference does it make where you learn?

Cudda: You can't worry about time gone by; that's water under the bridge.

Wudda: Well, if your parents had taken time to help you plan your life's work, you would be in a better place today.

IMAWISE: You used the time you had in the best way you knew how to at the time.

NEW THOUGHT

I honor the choices I've made in regard to how I spent my time, yesterday and today.

When I first saw my inner child, I did not know what to do for her or with her. I could see how hurt she was and I wanted to comfort her. I was overwhelmed by her feeling of abandonment. I also felt I should have listened to her much sooner than I did.

Shudda: What is this "inner child" thing? You are a grownup and you should act like one.

Cudda: You can't change the past, so why worry about that now?

Wudda: Life is unfair to all children. You can't reverse that now. Anyway, who says a small child lives inside of you?

IMAWISE: The child inside of you will let you know what she needs at all times. You can listen and act.

NEW THOUGHT

I listen to the needs of my inner
child in all situations.

May 31

I have given in to depression a number of times. Like others, I suppose, I thought a couple of times about ending my life. It just seemed sometimes that life was not worth living. That thought usually scared me enough to get help.

Shudda: Taking one's life is a sin. You must not think about that. Never, ever!

Cudda: What if everybody did this all at once? Try harder to find a way out.

Wudda: You can't take your own life because it isn't really yours to begin with.

IMAWISE: At times it seems like life is not worth living. This is your cue to make changes.

NEW THOUGHT

Even during bad times I can make
the changes I need to make.

JUNE

Blame is
only useful when
I do not want to
see the part
I didn't do.

June 1

I have heard all my life that I need to take care of my body. I have also heard all my life that for one reason or another, my body is not quite what it should be. It doesn't look like this model or that model. I learned to be ashamed about my body parts.

Shudda: The body is the temple of the Spirit. Best not to talk about it.

Cudda: It is hopeless with all the work you do to try to change it now.

Wudda: You will be all alone if you accept your body as it is, and you may be the subject of laughter if you don't look "right."

IMAWISE: The body is the temple of the Spirit and it deserves the best care you can offer.

NEW THOUGHT

I make the choices that either honor
or dishonor my body.

In keeping with this idea about loving one's body, I am learning not to compare myself with others. It is very hard to break this habit, as it has been a part of living for as long as I can remember. Constant comparison with other bodies used to feel necessary; now it feels like a ball and chain.

Shudda: How can you know if you measure up if you don't look outside yourself for answers?

Cudda: You just have to try harder to like who and what you are.

Wudda: You may lose some friends who will wonder what is going on with you.

IMAWISE: Comparing usually means falling short. Falling short means hurt. What can you do instead?

NEW THOUGHT

I look at the occasions when I choose to compare myself with others to see what is behind my need to do that.

Learning to love myself entails saying kind things to myself. Doing that felt false at first. But saying these things gives me the chance to examine how I really feel about myself.

Shudda: You should love others, too—not just yourself.

Cudda: It is hopeless to put yourself first. Try it and see. No one will like it.

Wudda: If I were you, I'd give up on others and realize that loving yourself just can't be done, either.

IMAWISE: Loving yourself is what was intended for you. It is a practice that heals.

NEW THOUGHT

I am healing with every loving
thought I give myself.

I know what to do to take proper care of myself. I know the importance of good food, sleep, exercise and psychological well-being. I look back on the years when I did not know what to do and wish I could have taken better care of myself over the long haul.

Shudda: Proper is as proper does.

Cudda: What if that were all you had to do—worry about proper care? Then what would others see—a selfish person, eh?

Wudda: With so many needs around you, it is really hard to take some time to care for yourself now, isn't it?

IMAWISE: Proper care of yourself is possible by the choices you make.

NEW THOUGHT

I choose to take good care of myself.

Years of taking care of others has prompted me always to be aware of the needs of others first. Even now, I find myself very aware of the needs of strangers. In the same moment I am likely to forget my own. Being a caregiver to others while ignoring my own needs was a role I played for so long that recovery will likely take just as long.

Shudda: Treat others the way you would want to be treated.

Cudda: What kind of world would we have if we all put ourselves first?

Wudda: You will find it simply impossible to put self first. It will cost you dearly.

IMAWISE: When you love yourself first, you demonstrate the best example of the Golden Rule.

NEW THOUGHT

In loving myself first, I am
able to love others.

I've spent years and years worrying over this, that and the other. When I had free time, worry took over. When there was joy, worry robbed the moment. When there was contentment, worry came and reminded me that the sense of contentment could go at any time.

Shudda: Best to be prepared for the worst. Then you are ready when it gets here.

Cudda: You could give up worrying, but then you'd be knocked off your feet when the worst comes . . . and it always does.

Wudda: You can't get help from others about this worry thing because it's up to you to use your faith.

IMAWISE: Feelings come and feelings go. Worry is a choice that can be changed at any moment.

NEW THOUGHT

I can free myself from worry
at any moment.

While I loved being able to help others and learned how to do that well, there was a longing in my soul to be doing something else. At a meeting about my first book, I worked with a co-author who did not want to work on the book. Exasperated, I left and went to a museum of modern art in that town.

Shudda: You quit? Now what does that say about you?

Cudda: This is hopeless. How do you think you will ever get anything published?

Wudda: Do you expect someone else to do the work?

IMAWISE: Longing for something else to do was a clue. Did you get it?

NEW THOUGHT

When I long for something, I can use
that feeling to help me understand
my needs at that time.

I was a very angry teenager with no safe way to vent that anger. I felt a rage—a fury inside of me that just wouldn't quit. It would well up inside me, and the only person there to hear it was my grandmother. To this day, I wish I could make amends to her.

Shudda: Yelling at an elder? Do you ever listen at church?

Cudda: You could have stifled yourself. She didn't need that..

Wudda: So you were angry; who isn't? What right did you have to take it out on her?

IMAWISE: You made a mistake. You lived through it. What did you learn from it?

NEW THOUGHT

I make every effort to tend to
my mistakes as I become
aware of them.

I even feel the same way about my younger brother. He started life with many difficulties—what my parents called "strikes against him." I felt a huge sense of sadness for him. I remember wishing that I could take on his problems so he could have a fair chance.

Shudda: You just have to love him no matter what and help him no matter what.

Cudda: No matter what, no matter what, no matter what. . . .

Wudda: Even if it seems unfair to you, he has so many problems that you do not have, you can set yourself aside.

IMAWISE: Pity for another usually leads you to assume undue responsibility for the happiness of that person.

NEW THOUGHT

I choose to see others
as capable.

I think of offering myself and my gifts to my Higher Power—as a last resort. It is the very last thing I think of . . . along with prayer and gratitude.

Shudda: Now see, that's what's wrong with you. Thinking of God last always gets you in trouble.

Cudda: Your outlook on life is simply hopeless.

Wudda: Just how far do you expect to get if God is not on your side?

IMAWISE: Offering yourself to God is the best gift you can give. You can do that anytime and God will honor it.

NEW THOUGHT

I can offer myself to the Creator
at any time I choose.

Gratitude is something I feel when the situation is so big that it is impossible to miss what my Higher Power has done. Then I find it easy to be grateful. Other times, especially in times when I struggle, gratitude is set aside for worrying and making plans.

Shudda: Be grateful all the time. You are able to if you can set your selfish desires aside.

Cudda: If you are not grateful, you are likely to lose that which means most to you.

Wudda: If you refuse to be grateful, the powers that be will surely rock your boat.

IMAWISE: Choosing to be grateful changes your outlook at any time.

NEW THOUGHT

Being grateful is a choice that can
lead me to my highest good.

No matter how much attention I give to my own healing work, I still feel that I have never worked hard enough on my own issues. Since there is always more work to be done on one's issues, I find it hard to rest and appreciate the work I have done.

Shudda: You spend too much time on yourself, and it's no wonder that you find it hard to rest. Guilt, guilt. . . .

Cudda: You can't ever let up on your own issues. There's so much more to do. . . .

Wudda: Others have really caused you a lot of problems over the years, so this is a massive cleanup operation. . . .

IMAWISE: True growth has moments of work and moments of rest.

NEW THOUGHT

I can rest and work as I grow.

I left an intolerable work environment without making excuses. I did not explain myself, even though my reasons for leaving were both ethical and understandable. This was a first for me—not explaining what I did.

Shudda: Now what would others think? You must explain your actions so that others will understand you.

Cudda: You're in trouble now, kid. They are likely to come to your house and wear you out.

Wudda: You have done the impossible. I didn't think you'd be comfortable leaving without explanation.

IMAWISE: There are times when leaving is the only acceptable answer.

NEW THOUGHT

When I choose to leave, it is because
I have decided it is the right move.

In many situations, I have spent long hours studying what others are doing. I have spent far less time finding my own way, even though this way has proved to be much more pleasing.

Shudda: I say check in with others; otherwise, you will lose touch with what's going on around you.

Cudda: Losing touch may mean you will look odd, even crazy, to others.

Wudda: Others can be very convincing, can't they?

IMAWISE: When you make your own path, you heal yourself and use your potential. You can find the way to your highest good.

NEW THOUGHT

When I choose to find my own path,
I find what I need to heal myself
and unlock my potential.

There have been a couple of instances in which I took unpopular stands against unfair treatment and found that I also had to burn my bridges at those same moments. I found that some others who cared little about the stands I took looked rather menacing.

Shudda: See what standing up for your beliefs gets you?

Cudda: Now you can worry about what they think.

Wudda: The reason they wouldn't stand up is that they feel threatened by others in control. When you stood up, they felt threatened.

IMAWISE: Standing up for your beliefs means that others may not like what you say or do. It is part of the process of standing up.

NEW THOUGHT

When I choose to stand up for my principles, I can also adjust my expectations of others.

I study problems. In any situation, I can assess what's unfair, askew or out of synch. I focus on the negative—at least I've made a career out of "correction." There were many, many silver linings that I missed. Today, I spend time looking for the silver linings.

Shudda: You must be ready for the worst, and focusing on the negatives helps you to get ready.

Cudda: Thinking about what could happen is the best defense.

Wudda: Seeing the gray clouds long before they get here will help you reach your dreams.

IMAWISE: Seeing both the clouds and silver linings leads to a healthy attitude.

NEW THOUGHT

I pay attention to the potential good
and the potential harm in
any situation I face.

Never feeling like I fit in meant that I left many jobs. This was often against the advice of trusted friends and colleagues. Each time, I went through an adjustment period when I felt I should have stayed at my old job.

Shudda: Yes, dearie, moving around so much does not look good on the old résumé, now does it?

Cudda: It makes you look unstable—incapable of adjusting to your surroundings.

Wudda: What others think about this is important because after all, they *are* your "bread and butter."

IMAWISE: You can trust your judgment about where and how long to be in any one place. No matter where you are or what you are doing, the Creator guides you.

NEW THOUGHT

I am learning to trust the
decisions I make.

I've long wanted to change the way my body looked. I dreamed for the will to have cosmetic surgery. I waited so long that it became necessary for my health to have this surgery. When I did, it was my first real surgical experience. I was terrified.

Shudda: God gave you the body you have. You don't need to change it.

Cudda: Having cosmetic surgery, even for a medical reason, is just too dangerous. Think about what could happen.

Wudda: Well, you can blame others if something goes wrong, and then sue them.

IMAWISE: This kind of experience does bring on fear. You can call on your Higher Power for help.

NEW THOUGHT

In all situations, I choose to think first about help from the Creator.

With many years in my field behind me, and years of good service, I still find that I long to develop other skills. Most of these skills have nothing to do with my work as a caregiver. I would like them to fit together, but most of the time they do not.

Shudda: Why can't you just be happy with what you have?

Cudda: If you don't appreciate what you have been able to do and learn, you will lose it.

Wudda: There are reasons why you can't do everything you want to do; not enough hours in the day, for one.

IMAWISE: You can make changes in your life and develop the skills you want at any time.

NEW THOUGHT

I remember my grandmother chose
to start painting at age 95. I can
start over many times.

Caught up in the lives of others, I have taken only a few brief trips to be with Nature. Though I love animals, I spend only rare moments with them. Here in Wyoming, we live among Nature. It is not uncommon to have deer, antelope, even a moose in your yard. My love of Nature is brought home to me here.

Shudda: You should not put Nature or creatures before God.

Cudda: You could have spent more time with Nature if you wanted to.

Wudda: There was never enough time to stop and do this. There are so many people with so many problems.

IMAWISE: Nature, in all her forms, is a gift of the Creator. You can choose to stop at any time to enjoy her gifts.

NEW THOUGHT

Today I take in my surroundings.
I see deer, antelope and other
gifts from my Creator.

I am always in a hurry, and it seems to me that nothing I do is ever on the time schedule that I want. Things should have been done yesterday or begun sooner. I set an impossible schedule of things to do and berate myself when I do not finish sooner than I expected.

Shudda: Busy is as busy does. Stay with it!

Cudda: You need to try harder to get things done on time.

Wudda: Being on time is just good manners. If you are early and you have done more work than anyone else, everyone will be so impressed.

IMAWISE: There is no magical pace and no need to beat others to the punch. You become a human "doing" rather than a human being when you feel the need to outdo others.

NEW THOUGHT

I choose a pace that helps me
reach my goals comfortably.

It seems to me that everyone's hair is long. As a child, I yearned for long braids. My hair was cut against my will. My choice—if someone had asked me—would have been to leave it long. Today I still wish for something other than what I have.

Shudda: A woman's hair is her crowning glory.

Cudda: What can you really do about all that now?

Wudda: So, they gave you a hard time about your hair a long time ago. What does that have to do with you now?

IMAWISE: It is important to be pleased with your appearance. The importance of your hair is also a key to healing the hurts of your past.

NEW THOUGHT

I see a hurt from the past and
I move to heal it now.

I long to understand other cultures and the people of those cultures. Even as a little girl, I longed to be friends with others and understand how they lived. I longed to live with people of other cultures so that I would know firsthand how life is for them.

Shudda: You can just imagine traveling to see them. Doing it would be dangerous.

Cudda: What if you spent all your time thinking about these other people and never got the chance to go see them?

Wudda: You don't have enough money to do all the traveling you really want to do.

IMAWISE: To wonder is normal and can lead you to understand others who are different from you.

NEW THOUGHT

I can trust my interest in others
and learn much from them.

I look back on a time when I could have chosen to travel abroad and found that it took more courage than I had at the time. I wish I had found the courage to travel in Europe as a teenager, when it was more affordable.

Shudda: You can learn about those people by reading about them. It is dangerous for a woman to travel alone.

Cudda: You could find the adventure you want by reading or watching videos.

Wudda: If your family had taught you to trust yourself, this conversation would be about adventure—not danger.

IMAWISE: It is natural to be curious about how others live. The courage to travel and explore comes from doing it.

NEW THOUGHT

Adventure is a gift
I can give myself.

I longed for the approval of others for so many years that I often volunteered to do things that others would not, just to stand out in the crowd. I gained much appreciation for doing jobs that others would not touch.

Shudda: If you have a lot, you must give a lot.

Cudda: If you fail to use your gifts, you will lose them.

Wudda: If you don't do your part, someone else will get there first and do it for you.

IMAWISE: Getting approval is a risky business. It sets you up for highs and lows, based on other people's views of you.

NEW THOUGHT

I look to myself for approval
and for my next step.

When I looked for answers, I looked in earnest to everyone but myself. In the last five years, I've decided I can lead myself and do okay.

Shudda: You need a leader who has sound spiritual thinking; keep looking.

Cudda: Just look a little more; there is someone who will lead you.

Wudda: You need to separate yourself from others who do not think as you do.

IMAWISE: Look inside and you will find a treasure from your Creator.

NEW THOUGHT

When I choose to look inside,
I do find treasure.

Now that I know that the answers I need are inside of me, I feel I should have looked there earlier. It is so simple to look within. Why didn't I think of that?

Shudda: I still think that others who have more knowledge are the ones you need to talk to.

Cudda: Yes, and if you keep trying to find the "right" people, you'll end up much more satisfied when you do.

Wudda: This search will feel impossible from time to time. You have to find the answers alone.

IMAWISE: This search can begin and end all in the same moment. Look inside.

NEW THOUGHT

I can choose to look inside anytime I need
to. The need to hurry or find
an "expert" is an illusion.

The bank account is low, always has been low, and is never full enough to suit my security needs. No matter how much effort I put into religiously saving, the account falls short of an amount I think I should have to be safe.

Shudda: A penny saved is a penny earned. These days you need to save all the pennies you can.

Cudda: Correct! There are many rainy days ahead.

Wudda: And retirement . . . what's your plan for retirement? Social Security will not pay.

IMAWISE: Always falling short means you can never catch up, and yet it keeps you trying too hard.

NEW THOUGHT

I can make myself safe by having faith,
which leads me to right action,
even in financial matters.

My parents always instructed me to save for "rainy days." I became caught up in the power of spending as one of the only ways I could feel powerful in my dysfunctional family. There was either feast in the bank account (much saving) or famine (excessive spending). I learned no healthy balance between the two.

Shudda: Becoming a spendthrift is sure to lead to disaster.

Cudda: Why do you think you need so many new things? This will defeat your best efforts at saving in less than a heartbeat.

Wudda: If I were you, I'd just live a minimal existence and save every available penny for the disaster that is sure to come.

IMAWISE: You can learn a healthy way to use money.

NEW THOUGHT

I can create the relationship I want
with the money I have.

Another lesson passed on to me by my parents was the need to stay put and not explore my surroundings. Though we traveled, rare was the time I was allowed to explore what really interested me, unless it also interested one of my parents. I learned to please my parents well by ignoring what I found fascinating.

Shudda: Honor your parents, as they are older than you and you won't have them around forever.

Cudda: Right. When they are dead, you can explore what you like.

Wudda: They never let themselves explore what they wanted, so why are you any different?

IMAWISE: Exploring what fascinates you allows you to grow, heal and find joy on your journey.

NEW THOUGHT

To be healthy, I need to explore
my own interests.

189

JULY

The reasons
things can't be done
are in fact the traps
I have learned to
set for myself.

July 1

For years I lived a sheltered life, almost comatose, in fact. Now after confronting that way of living, I seek every day to change it. I am open to new things and new experiences, not wanting to miss much. Looking back keeps me wishing I had tried more new things.

Shudda: Now those years are past. What can you do? Just think about something pleasant.

Cudda: It is hopeless to think about changing these things. You can't turn the clock back now.

Wudda: That wasted time is really the fault of family who didn't help or show interest in you.

IMAWISE: The lessons of the past are learned. The most important thing now is to learn today.

NEW THOUGHT

I learned what I could from the moments of my past; my focus is now.

Upon emerging from that sheltered life, almost anything seemed scary. Anything new and different was intriguing . . . but also seemed dangerous. I approached everything with an uncertainty about whether I could do it or if I would look foolish trying.

Shudda: Most things that are new have some danger attached to them. Best not to try!

Cudda: If you worry about them now, you will not want to try anything new.

Wudda: Again, if you had had the support that kids really need, you'd be much farther down the road than you are now.

IMAWISE: Feel your fears and release them as you try new things.

NEW THOUGHT

My fears about trying new things are real.
I do not let them stop me.

July 3

Once I had a taste of adventure, such as scuba diving in the warm waters of the Caribbean, I wanted MORE. I felt more alive than I had ever felt before, and the adventure pumped the natural level of adrenaline through my body. I was free to explore and see all that interested me!

Shudda: Do you know what kind of danger you are in when you explore?

Cudda: Yes, don't go overboard. There are so many dangers you do not know about.

Wudda: If you do too much, there will be no one there to help you because everyone will be so jealous.

IMAWISE: Feeling a sense of adventure is a normal human experience. Enjoy it and learn to balance it with the rest of your life.

NEW THOUGHT

My life can be an adventure and I can
learn to balance adventure with
the rest of my life.

Right away, I felt the freedom and exhilaration of traveling alone. I left the United States, traveled in Asia and fell head-over-heels for the differences in the way people live on this planet. My childhood instincts were correct: I found others fascinating. I felt a sense of awe for how others created their lifestyles, especially those with meager resources.

Shudda: You are really off the deep end. Those people you want to visit are violent, you know.

Cudda: Yes, something could happen to you and no one would ever know it.

Wudda: What would you do if, while you were doing all this traveling, you ended up in jail for no reason?

IMAWISE: Traveling to see how others live can be done in a safe and reasonable way.

NEW THOUGHT

I take good care of myself when
I am visiting unfamiliar places.

My time in Asia was thrilling, but I knew nothing of my own heritage. My family heritage had never been discussed much, except to say that we were Irish, German, Swedish and Scottish. I longed to know more and began a genealogy using historical records. I learned where my family originated and when they arrived in the New World. I felt connected.

Shudda: This is something that your parents told you about, but you never listened.

Cudda: You could have known this all along, except you were not interested.

Wudda: You needed to listen to what your parents knew so that you could get the story right.

IMAWISE: What you understand about your heritage is your own business. You choose whether you will look into it or not.

NEW THOUGHT

I learn about myself and my heritage as I see the need.

I felt that there was something missing inside me, so I worked extra hard and overtime to cover up for that loss. I never let anyone see me down and I sought approval from everyone. I found dozens of ways to get that approval. I ended up in counseling because this became a way of life.

Shudda: It's easier on you if you agree with everyone around you.

Cudda: Others can't change who you are. You have to do that.

Wudda: If you can't do it all by yourself, then what good are you?

IMAWISE: Change is done alone and with others. We all need one another from time to time.

NEW THOUGHT

I change by helping myself and letting others help me as well.

If I had known about my talents in the visual arts, I would have pursued them. I would not have ignored them, as my family did. Starting at about age three or four, I wrote poems and produced good art. The fact that it was ignored first by the family, and then by me, deeply saddens me.

Shudda: Your parents did the best they could. Give it up!

Cudda: If they could have supported you, how might that have changed your life today?

Wudda: Blaming them is one thing you might do to remember who is responsible for what you lacked. Never forget!

IMAWISE: And now that you recognize other abilities, you also have some new decisions to make about how to use them.

NEW THOUGHT

I see my personal abilities and try to
make the most of them today.

Quantum leaps have been the story of my personal growth. These have been followed by long and boring plateaus. The results are highs and lows and periods of exhaustion. I long for small measured steps.

Shudda: You can't redo anything, so why even think about it?

Cudda: You are just making this up about leaps and plateaus. No one really lives that way.

Wudda: If you ask me, others put a lot of roadblocks in front of you—big ones that you had to move in order to go on.

IMAWISE: How you grow is your unique approach to life.

NEW THOUGHT

I grow in my own way. I can learn
to honor that path.

Quantum leaps require leaps of faith. I look back and see many leaps and wonder still how they transpired without doing me in. I wish I had trusted myself more to be able to support myself.

Shudda: O ye of little faith!

Cudda: Yes, where is the mustard seed of faith when you need it?

Wudda: I can see why you wondered. Most of your hopes and dreams are really out of your reach.

IMAWISE: You had just the amount of faith you needed when you needed it.

NEW THOUGHT

I use my faith to the best of my
ability at any given time.

I often wish for a closer relationship to Mother Earth and all her creatures. I long to be closer to the animals in particular. They seem to be precious, precious creatures of the Creator and feel like sisters and brothers to me.

Shudda: They do now, do they? Animals are not as important as the people in your life, you know.

Cudda: Look at all you can do for the human world, and let the animals take care of themselves.

Wudda: They would refuse your help anyway, because they are scared of humans.

IMAWISE: It is wise to see the connectedness of all things.

NEW THOUGHT

I see and love the connection between myself and all that is.

I often conclude that I could have offered more help to others than I did. I have not seen this as co-dependency. I saw this as my duty. It was the way I mattered in the world I knew, especially since I did not matter to myself.

Shudda: Work, for the night is coming!

Cudda: So now you don't need to do anything for others?

Wudda: If they refuse your help, then what will you do? Move on to someone who will receive it?

IMAWISE: You can learn to live with limits. Good boundaries are vital for good health.

NEW THOUGHT

I can say "No" when I need
to set a limit.

I hated being alone, living alone and doing things alone when I was younger. After my divorce, I learned to live by myself and take care of my own needs. Others often thought I was sad about being alone, when really I'd learned to enjoy it.

Shudda: How selfish and full of denial you are! No one really likes being alone.

Cudda: If you really like living alone, maybe you'll love dying alone.

Wudda: Then you can't blame others who reached out to you when you chose not to respond.

IMAWISE: Learning to be alone and comfortable with yourself is a healthy step in personal growth.

NEW THOUGHT

Learning to live by myself was both an adventure and a healthy thing to do.

I found many ways to enjoy time alone. I just found it very hard to convince others that they did not need to take care of me, especially at holidays.

Shudda: That's just good denial. No one likes to be alone for the holidays.

Cudda: That could have been dangerous, even depressing.

Wudda: Think of all the people you've turned down and whose feelings you've hurt.

IMAWISE: Being alone is a choice that is often misunderstood by others. You can choose to explain it or not.

NEW THOUGHT

I learned to be comfortable alone
throughout all seasons.

People often convinced me that I needed others, when I really felt quite comfortable alone. At those times, I wished for a better relationship with my parents. If I had better connections with them, then I wouldn't be alone, I reasoned.

Shudda: See what you have done? What kind of religious person would have poor connections with her parents?

Cudda: If you had only tried harder all these years, things would be better for you with them.

Wudda: Yes, and you wouldn't feel alone.

IMAWISE: Trust your own feelings. They are right for you.

NEW THOUGHT

I can choose to trust even the
worst of my feelings.

I have found the need to get others' approval. I wanted them to agree with me because that made my world more comfortable. I did not feel threatened when we all agreed.

Shudda: Agreement means safety.

Cudda: If you disagree, that could lead to big conflicts and the people you love will leave you.

Wudda: You would be all alone to face this big old world. You don't want that, now, do you?

IMAWISE: Disagreement does not mean the end of things. You can learn that it means something needs to be worked out.

NEW THOUGHT

Disagreement teaches me to work out
things with those around me.

While people in other lands have long fascinated me, it was how extraordinary their lives were that intrigued me most. I learned that parts of their daily lives were as difficult for them as parts of mine were for me. I wanted to learn more about their daily lives in order to understand them.

Shudda: Of course you would forget that others have problems, too.

Cudda: Yes, you could set aside what these people could do for you or how they might entertain you to really learn something about them.

Wudda: This is a great opportunity to learn, and you almost blew it.

IMAWISE: We are drawn to what fascinates us about others, and then we learn the more mundane aspects of their lives.

NEW THOUGHT

Fascination with others leads me to new understanding of how they live.

Looking back over 20 years of a career in the helping field, I long to have done one more thing. I long to have spent more time with art, especially visual representations of art. I understand it now as the conscience of a society. I long now to have been a part of that all these years.

Shudda: You can't turn the clock back.
Cudda: If you had prioritized your life better, you could have done that.
Wudda: It's just a dream you can let go of now as you age.

IMAWISE: You can reach for any dream in you that is still unfulfilled.

NEW THOUGHT

At any age, I can choose my dreams
and what to do about them.

At age four, I was fascinated with crayons and clay. I found ways to sneak out of the house and play with both. Mother let it slip that my kindergarten teachers thought I was, as she put it, "years ahead of herself in art." No one did anything to support that idea. I wish now that I had appreciated myself even at that young age and then insisted on some support.

Shudda: Your parents could not give you the attention you think you needed.

Cudda: Yes: they were hard on each other and that is why your little needs were sometimes set aside.

Wudda: This is a childish wish! Get a real life!

IMAWISE: Whatever talent you have not used can still be put to work.

NEW THOUGHT

A dream is only dead
if I let it be.

I turned my artistic talent into something that was appreciated by my family. I taught myself to sew, and I sewed entire wardrobes. I learned all about color, texture and design that way. That was in full view of others in my family, who appreciated it because it often helped them. I could not sew enough, and wished for more and more.

Shudda: As long as your talent serves someone besides yourself, that is what we are here to do.

Cudda: What else could you have done with your time to put it to better use?

Wudda: If you have to do things alone, you might as well serve others.

IMAWISE: The talent was preserved.

NEW THOUGHT

I have talents that wait
for me to use them.

In terms of finances, I know nothing about how to plan for the future. I find that a bit scary, each year as I grow older. I know of the need to save and plan now. I know I should have planned years ago for this and now wish I had.

Shudda: If you fail to plan, you plan to fail. This is surely true in the case of finances.

Cudda: You started several good plans and then let go for silly things, like art—art that never sells.

Wudda: Again, this is one of those things that your folks should have told you about and, of course, did not.

IMAWISE: You can make the plans you need now for your retirement, which includes your dreams.

NEW THOUGHT

I can take care of myself as I grow
older by making plans now.

It seems I am out of the information loop as far as knowing how, when and what investments to make. I see others getting ahead because they have access to this information. I'm still in the same financial rut.

Shudda: This is something you should have asked your grandfather about. He was a whiz!

Cudda: You could have tried harder all along, instead of setting the priorities you had.

Wudda: Still, others have had so many breaks that you have not had.

IMAWISE: If you want to learn about investments now, you can.

NEW THOUGHT

Whatever I decide I need to learn,
I can find a way to learn it.

I have several bad habits that ruffle my feathers. I do not smoke or drink. I just worry obsessively, check and double-check on things that are important to me.

Shudda: All that checking keeps you on your toes.

Cudda: What if one time, you ran off and left the back door standing wide open? Then what?

Wudda: Yes, then what would you do when the unjust of the world helped themselves to all you own?

IMAWISE: Bad habits are clues to what you still need to give yourself.

NEW THOUGHT

I can learn to change habits anytime
and let them teach me about the
extent of my own needs.

Addictions, I've learned, develop from a sense of shame. Shame is the master feeling, binding all others. Shame says to the person, "You are a mistake." The person believes that there is nothing that can reverse this feeling and so learns to live with it by "overdoing" something. I learned about my shame and my addictions to spending, clothing, caffeine and work.

Shudda: You should not feel shame for what God created.

Cudda: You could have figured this out much sooner and you'd be in a better place now.

Wudda: What's wrong with doing a little more of something, as long as you can handle it?

IMAWISE: Once you learn you have shame, you can heal it by coming out of hiding.

NEW THOUGHT

I let my sense of shame teach
me what I need to heal.

I've always had to be surrounded by beauty. So I looked for pretty places to live, and I did not care what it cost me. This obsession with pretty places kept me seeking better and better places to live, never being satisfied with what I had.

Shudda: You can't ever be grateful, can you?

Cudda: If you could be grateful for what you have, you could also learn to live in one place.

Wudda: No one is going to help you figure this one out. You have to do it alone.

IMAWISE: This attraction to beauty is a clue about your real needs. Find out what it means.

NEW THOUGHT

What attracts me can also teach
me about myself.

I found all kinds of work to do as a teenager and as an adult. Most of the work I chose to do at either time, I did to please someone else. I never stopped to ask myself about the kind of work I might *like* to do.

Shudda: Still having problems when you please others, I see.

Cudda: What if everyone quit helping each other, as you are thinking about doing?

Wudda: And no one else ever asked you, either. So part of this is your parents' fault.

IMAWISE: You can still change the work you do and make it more pleasing to you.

NEW THOUGHT

When I want to make changes in
my work life, I can do this.

I should have listened more carefully to others' opinions about the kinds of work I could do. I saw many career counselors over the years and let them guide me. Still, I chose to make many career changes when things seemed to no longer fit.

Shudda: You should have listened to the experts, right?

Cudda: Stay with the career that makes the most money and gives you the most power and prestige.

Wudda: What would you do if you chose something that would not make you any money, like art?

IMAWISE: You made changes when you saw the need. These lessons are vital.

NEW THOUGHT

I can make changes in my work
life and survive all of them.

I wish now that someone had been available to me to hear the feelings I had about my need to find the right work. Even if someone had, I am not sure I would have been able or willing to express what I truly felt. I learned to bury deeply the desires of my own heart until I was surrounded by safety.

Shudda: Why should your parents or anyone else try to help if you are not going to be honest with them anyway?

Cudda: You could have given them one more chance.

Wudda: What would happen to us if everyone gave up, as you did?

IMAWISE: You buried your true feelings in order to preserve them. Make sure your surroundings are safe now, and you can share them.

NEW THOUGHT

I share my true feelings only when
the setting is safe to do that.

218

Worry and concern have been constant companions for as long as I can remember. In all my travels, they have been there, robbing each moment of its beauty. When I realized this, I was 40 years old and found myself wondering about all the beauty I had missed. I wished I had smelled more flowers along the way.

Shudda: When you worry, there are things to worry about.

Cudda: You could have tried to see God's beauty all around you, but you had no faith.

Wudda: You were too busy solving other people's problems.

IMAWISE: See the beauty. Take in all you can. There is so much to see and feel.

NEW THOUGHT

I begin each day by seeing beauty
all around me.

Somewhere along the line, I think I should have bought a house. Again, this was something that felt too big to handle. I did not attempt it because it was easier to rent than it was to set down roots. Now after 42 years of living in numerous places, I wish that I had bought my own home.

Shudda: See, you need to settle down somewhere. There's still lots of cheap housing.

Cudda: You could have had different priorities, lived like your family, had children, been normal—get the point?

Wudda: You can't really settle down anywhere because you would end up not fitting in, remember?

IMAWISE: You can learn whatever you need to learn about settling down and buying a house, if and when you are ready.

NEW THOUGHT

I will know when I am ready to settle down.
There is a place that will feel right to me.

If I had stayed in one place and settled into a solid job, I would have a house of my own. I moved a lot whenever I felt unsettled. I just could not stay in one place. Many people had seen that as a deficit in me. I have seen my life as one adventure after another.

Shudda: You need to pay attention to what they are saying about you.

Cudda: They could say that you are addicted to risk and that your life is unstable.

Wudda: Why is it that you have to do things alone all the time?

IMAWISE: Moving and changing have taught you important lessons you could not have learned any other way. You will know when to settle down.

NEW THOUGHT

I will know the right place and
time to settle down.

I was willing to experiment with many different kinds of jobs. I left jobs that did not fit with my sense of ethics. I left other jobs that were good but sucked the life out of me. I looked for what gave me the greatest sense of contentment.

Shudda: Contentment is having money in the bank.

Cudda: It is a solid retirement plan. You could have had concrete plans for your future.

Wudda: What can you do now? You are halfway there—with almost nothing, I might add.

IMAWISE: You learned what you learned and this was valuable. You still have all kinds of choices to make today.

NEW THOUGHT

I choose what fits for me with
faith in my Higher Power.

AUGUST

Choices and
problems that arise
from decisions
are both powerful and
forgiving teachers.

There are days when I wish I had spent more time with children—other people's children and my own. I seldom let myself off the hook for this, preferring to believe that more time meant better time. Sometimes I question if what was right for me was also right for them.

Shudda: You can't turn back the hands of time now. You should have thought about that before you made your choices.

Cudda: The worst thing that can happen is that they will follow bad examples that they see in the world because you showed them nothing better.

Wudda: They will blame you for the hurt in their lives, and you'll have to get used to that.

IMAWISE: Whatever you did at any time was the best you knew how to do.

NEW THOUGHT

I did what I could and for whatever
mistakes I made, I can now
choose to make amends.

I learned about positive stress and negative stress and the effects of both on humans and animals. I never saw myself as a stressed person until I looked at the events of my early life, right up until now. I found myself wishing that I had worked with it better and known more about how to treat my own body when it was under stress.

Shudda: You should take care of your body the way the experts suggest.

Cudda: What's going to happen to you if you don't?

Wudda: You have all these great hopes and dreams, and they'll go out the window.

IMAWISE: Now that you know about stress, you have new choices to make that can support good health.

NEW THOUGHT

This moment offers me a choice of
habits that support good health
and deal well with stress.

August 3

I can't remember when I last took a real lunch hour at work. When I worked for someone else, I just ate lunch at my desk or skipped it altogether. I never saw the real value of taking that break in the day. I was sure that my employers were impressed with my dedication.

Shudda: All work and no rest makes you a dull person.

Cudda: If you never take a break, you won't be as good as you could be at what you do.

Wudda: Well, there's just so much work to be done, and it's done better during the early part of the day.

IMAWISE: Taking a break is healthy and often necessary.

NEW THOUGHT

When I take a break in my day,
I return refreshed.

Many decisions I have made have been frowned upon by friends. Once I found that nine friends decided I had made a mistake, and they all turned their backs on me. I wondered if I'd made a serious blunder in my decision. It didn't occur to me that each friend might have had her own issues stirred up by what she saw in me.

Shudda: You should listen to people who love you. They have your best interests in mind.

Cudda: Now what can you do to get them back into your life?

Wudda: They have their own problems that get in the way of understanding.

IMAWISE: Their reactions are theirs; others won't always understand.

NEW THOUGHT

I let others have their own reactions.

I rarely encourage myself to cry. I prefer to keep my pain up in my head, where I can just "think" it through and analyze it to death. When I do cry, it is because all other avenues of expression are exhausted, and so am I.

Shudda: Just think pleasant thoughts.
Cudda: If you can't do it, you just can't.
Wudda: Sometimes it's just impossible to cry, so why try?

IMAWISE: If you can cry when you feel the urge, and keep at least some of this stuff out of your head, you can heal through your tears.

NEW THOUGHT

When I feel like crying I will let
myself do it in order to heal.

I jump in almost always where angels fear to tread. I do so, I think, in order to distinguish myself and feel important. It almost never occurred to me that others could benefit from learning their own lessons. It never once came to mind that I might be standing in their way.

Shudda: If you have the answers, it is important to share them with all the people of the world.

Cudda: Since you know so much, you are obligated to share what you know.

Wudda: No matter what the price is to you!

IMAWISE: There are times to help and times to step back and let others learn in their own ways.

NEW THOUGHT

I can learn when it is best to step in and help, and when others can better learn on their own.

I am learning that there are ways to share with others that do not include persuasion to my point of view. When ideas are being shared, I listen to learn new ways. Then I decide if I want to share what I know.

Shudda: Weren't you listening? If you have the answers, then you are obligated to share what you know.

Cudda: What if everybody who is educated held back what they know?

Wudda: People will just refuse your ideas a lot anyway, because like you, they will want to do it on their own.

IMAWISE: Sharing does not mean convincing; it means giving.

NEW THOUGHT

I can learn new ways to offer ideas
that involve listening to others.

I still find ways to blame others for my actions. It seems that I am quite accomplished at this. I look to the past for all my answers and I leave nothing to chance. Everything that is going on has a reason, and that reason has little to do with me. It has more to do with the shortcomings of others, both in the past and now.

Shudda: You can't blame others for your shortcomings. They can see yours and if they can't, God can.

Cudda: The only thing you can do here is try harder to see what is wrong.

Wudda: Right. And then try to fix it yourself. You can only fix this yourself.

IMAWISE: Blaming others was the only way out of a problem you felt you could not solve. Blaming can change to personal responsibility.

NEW THOUGHT

I can choose to blame or to
take personal responsibility.

I was afraid to take responsibility for my own actions. I was scared that I would go overboard with this and take on everyone else's as well. It did not occur to me that there could be healthy limits with this, too.

Shudda: Just think pleasant thoughts and quit trying to figure everything out.

Cudda: What if you just tried to make everything right—wouldn't that work?

Wudda: No one is going to help you with this, so you might as well get used to doing it on your own.

IMAWISE: You can learn the limits of responsibility for your actions by taking responsibility for your part only.

NEW THOUGHT

I learn the limits of responsibility
for my actions by taking
responsibility for my part.

I am 42 and now stand on my own two feet, for the most part. I wonder what took me so long. I think I can handle most things that I encounter and at the same time, I just can't imagine what took me so long to get to this point.

Shudda: It's that haughty little attitude that is sure to get you in big trouble.

Cudda: Big trouble! Big trouble!

Wudda: You will have to climb out of it on your own; there is no one to help.

IMAWISE: The feelings you have are real. It does feel as though it took a long time to get here. You can ask for help.

NEW THOUGHT

I can handle the feelings I have about
all the things that happen to me.
I get help when I need it.

I do not like regrets. They mean I forgot to do something really important. Over the years, I have made a mental list of things that I want to do before I pass over. I have done many of these things, and added other things to the list as well. One is to spend much quality time with my mate.

Shudda: And that you should. In fact, you should put him first.

Cudda: If you did that, you could not blame yourself later on for not spending time with him.

Wudda: To do that, all you have to do is let go of those silly dreams and goals you have, which aren't going to fly anyway.

IMAWISE: Make the most of the time that is given you with anyone you love.

NEW THOUGHT

I continue to make the most
of time that is given to me.

"They" say that grieving is a good thing. What they don't tell you is that no one really likes to be around people who are grieving. Also, if you start to cry, people want to comfort you so that you will stop. It's no wonder I have never grieved some of the losses I felt.

Shudda: Think about the good things in your life. Crying over spilt milk does not help now.

Cudda: If you cry, you will make me cry. Do you want that?

Wudda: You make such an ugly face when you cry. Would you just go somewhere by yourself?

IMAWISE: Grief is healthy, albeit uncomfortable and puzzling. It helps to move you forward.

NEW THOUGHT

When I need to grieve, I do so
for my own health.

235

I miss what others try to do for me so often that it really annoys me when I figure it out. Others do little things for me and because the things are little, they escape my notice. Then I am embarrassed and ashamed when I do figure it out.

Shudda: Always appreciate! Always appreciate!

Cudda: If you can't see it, try harder!

Wudda: If everyone missed these things, where would we all be?

IMAWISE: Slow down and see what others are trying to do for you and accept, if you can, their version of love.

NEW THOUGHT

I can slow myself to see the gifts
that others are offering me.

My partner is one person that I need to help and appreciate more. He is very helpful to me, and it seems that I have grown to expect it. I am slower to offer help, feeling, I think, that I will be overwhelmed as I was when I was a child. I find it hard to learn the balance between under- and over-helping.

Shudda: Why can't you just be a good helper? Who cares if you take on too much?

Cudda: Maybe you could make better excuses when you don't want to help.

Wudda: What good would it do to offer the incorrect amount of help? Just let him do it on his own.

IMAWISE: It is difficult to know when you are helping too much. All you can do is your best and that is usually enough.

NEW THOUGHT

I do my best with my partner.
I let go of trying to be a perfect mate.

Why do I worry all the time? My partner recently asked me to take a one-day vacation from all my worries. The idea of a vacation from worry was a real shock. What would I do if I wasn't worrying? I decided to try it anyway. How do you spell relief? L-E-T G-O!

Shudda: Now, when you quit thinking of others and what they want and need, do you know what happens?

Cudda: Just think: when you give up thinking about them, who will be there for them?

Wudda: Is there a real way out of worry for you? I do not think so.

IMAWISE: Letting go of worry means returning to faith in yourself and your Higher Power.

NEW THOUGHT

I can choose faith over worry.

So many imagined problems have led me to despair, long before they ever occurred—if, in fact, they ever did. For instance, I worried and felt desperate over my grandmother's death long before it ever happened. I wish I had tried to overcome my worrying.

Shudda: O ye of little faith, missy!

Cudda: It might be good to get ready for the worst because it is coming.

Wudda: What can you do about things you can't see, except worry?

IMAWISE: Overcoming is a step-by-step walk in faith. It is a choice you make one step at a time.

NEW THOUGHT

I choose to trust my Higher Power,
one step at a time.

I often think about the fun I would like to have if I could just get everything else done first. Unfortunately, "everything" means just that. Every little bit of work that I can think of must come first. Fun is usually the last thing on my mind.

Shudda: Life is a serious thing.

Cudda: If you do not take life seriously, the worst is bound to happen.

Wudda: You must watch out for this, if you are going to try to have fun at the same time.

IMAWISE: Fun is healthy. It is good to find a balance between fun and work.

NEW THOUGHT

I can find the right balance for myself between fun and everything else.

I am finding that I need to say what is bothering me at the time I am bothered by it. I have always been frightened of doing so, fearing that someone would react explosively and I would be overwhelmed and unable to handle it. Usually I found no explosion but instead, a way to clear the air.

Shudda: Best to keep quiet about how you really feel; no one cares, anyway.

Cudda: If you say what you feel, there will come an explosion, be it now or later.

Wudda: Then what would you do with everything in pieces? Would it be all your fault?

IMAWISE: If you can say what is on your mind and in your heart, you can stay healthy in each moment.

NEW THOUGHT

When I take care of my feelings
in the moment, I choose
health for myself.

After the fact, I saw that things came out alright. They always did, but I needed to know that they would. I could not just accept good outcome on blind faith; I needed signs and symbols that mattered to me.

Shudda: Now what kind of faith is that, that needs signs and symbols?

Cudda: This way is hopeless. You have to have faith at least the size of a mustard seed to get anywhere in this world.

Wudda: What would God say about your lack of faith?

IMAWISE: Signs and symbols help guide your faith. They are there to help you.

NEW THOUGHT

Signs and symbols help my
faith, not hinder it.

When I began to see that faith could be used in all situations, I also saw that faith could be used in creative ways. I saw that my faith was evidence of a Creative Source available to all people, if only they chose to use it.

Shudda: You should have seen this long ago. Look at how far ahead of you others are who use their faith.

Cudda: Think of where you could be now if you had only relied on your faith, as they have relied on theirs.

Wudda: If others in your life had helped you more, you would be like these other people.

IMAWISE: You are where and who you need to be. Longing to be someone else is a lack of faith.

NEW THOUGHT

I appreciate myself and the understanding
I have about my faith right now.

I found my own creativity to be a strangely powerful resource. I was afraid of it. I studied and tried to understand it on an intellectual level for a long time. Then I came to see that creativity was a sound spiritual force that could be used to manifest good. It is my choice how I use it.

Shudda: We need to use our faith in the ways that our leaders tell us.

Cudda: That's right. If you strike out on your own, no tellin' what will happen.

Wudda: If you are going to do these wild things with your faith, you need to hide what you are doing.

IMAWISE: Creativity is spiritual power, and you are right: what you do with it is up to you.

NEW THOUGHT

I choose to use my creative resource
for the highest good.

In our tiny house there are few things. If we have a lot of anything, it is art supplies. I have gathered and discarded, gathered and discarded things many times over the years. Now, in looking back, I realize that things did not really matter all that much. What mattered more was how I treated others.

Shudda: You should have known that all along.

Cudda: No need to try to redo this; you really could have tried harder all that time with all those things.

Wudda: You couldn't get all those things back together anyway. So what does it matter?

IMAWISE: Things were once easier for you to be with. Now you can choose to be different about things and people.

NEW THOUGHT

I let go of my need for things.
My focus is how I treat
myself and others.

245

I wish I had made better use of all the free time I received over the years. Mostly, I wish that I had discovered more about my environment. I wish I had explored more in Nature and had more adventures as a younger person in the natural world.

Shudda: Can't you ever be happy with what was?

Cudda: There's nothing that can be done about all that now.

Wudda: Face up to it. You blew off a lot of time that was given to you. Time is precious. Time is money.

IMAWISE: You explored to the extent that you felt comfortable.

NEW THOUGHT

I explore more today and I make sure
that my need for adventure
with Nature is met.

When I went into business, I failed miserably at almost everything I did. I was used to pleasing others when I worked for them, and they had already faced the tough decisions of their business. They made right and wrong decisions and survived both.

Shudda: Going into business for yourself is just too dangerous for a woman your age.

Cudda: What you don't know will eat you alive.

Wudda: When you fail, and you *will* fail, you can just blame it on the economy or on those people who shut you out.

IMAWISE: Whatever happens to you in your own business is a lesson.

NEW THOUGHT

I can learn from the lessons
I face and fail.

I did not protect myself in starting my own business. I did not educate myself in marketing or sales, although I knew the content of the work very well. I felt a lot of shame when it didn't go well.

Shudda: It's just like I told you. Why don't you listen?

Cudda: You haven't seen the worst yet. It's coming, though!

Wudda: If you are going to make it work at all, you have to do the whole thing alone. No one is going to help you.

IMAWISE: What did you learn from all this? Were the lessons the ones you needed?

NEW THOUGHT

I learn from all the events in my life.
I learn from failure and success.

When entering a new setting, I usually forget that there are rules that I do not know. I just plunge right in and begin doing what seems right to me, until someone who "knows better" straightens me out. I usually feel ashamed.

Shudda: As well you should!

Cudda: What if everybody jumped in where they wanted to, like you?

Wudda: We'd have a real mess—maybe even a serious accident!

IMAWISE: You can slow down and learn the rules, and then take part with equal zest.

NEW THOUGHT

Learning the rules means I can show
respect to others wherever I am.

I often left disagreements having given in to the other party, as if I was afraid of him or her. I often gave up much more than I wanted, preferring to soothe the other party. In many instances now, I know when I should have argued my point.

Shudda: Arguing is not the happy way. The important thing is to keep everyone else happy.

Cudda: Yes, everyone else must be happy.

Wudda: You can't blame anyone but yourself if you give up on this idea.

IMAWISE: Standing up for yourself is vital to your good health.

NEW THOUGHT

I invite good health when I stand
up for my own beliefs.

I lived a closed-off life for many years. I saw others doing things and trying new ideas and it awakened me to my own potential. I came alive slowly, still wishing I had experimented with my career and interests.

Shudda: What is wrong with what you've done with your life?

Cudda: You could have asked your parents to help you find other things to do.

Wudda: Your hopes and dreams are already out the window. Don't you know that?

IMAWISE: Now that you are awake to your potential, the choices are endless and all yours.

NEW THOUGHT

I can choose to use my potential
to pursue the dream
of my choice.

I did not make good money decisions for most of my adult life until now. I overlooked free services that were available to me, preferring to spend money and buy what I needed. I accumulated many things that I eventually outgrew and shed. There were many seasons of shedding. There was a continual upkeep of things and neglect of my soul.

Shudda: Unto whom much is given, much is expected.

Cudda: The reason why you had so much stuff was because you worked hard enough to deserve it.

Wudda: That is right. They asked so much of you that you deserved to have all those nice things.

IMAWISE: First, take care of your soul, the most precious gift of the Creator.

NEW THOUGHT

My first concern is with my
personal care and safety.

For many years I worked without a vacation and no days or nights off. If I wasn't working, I was getting ready for work. Work was the center of my life. It wasn't until last year that I realized this was an addiction. I now try to find a balance between the leisure pastimes I enjoy and my work.

Shudda: Work is good for the soul.

Cudda: It can't hurt you. Play is for kids and you are no kid anymore.

Wudda: If you want to have fun, you can have two weeks out of the year, after putting in 50 weeks of hard labor.

IMAWISE: There needs to be a balance between work and fun.

NEW THOUGHT

I can find a balance of work
and fun each day.

At 42, I am finally doing what I want to do. How about that for taking awhile to become satisfied? I often tell myself there must have been a shorter route.

Shudda: The shortest route to anything is full of barriers and evil things.

Cudda: Just think—you could still be dealing with all of them!

Wudda: And if this is your dream, others surely would have stolen it from you long ago.

IMAWISE: The route you took is a good one, full of lessons learned and wisdom gained.

NEW THOUGHT

Everything that happens to me
on my path works toward
my highest good.

SEPTEMBER

Hopes and dreams
are lived one step
at a time.

I left many healing and religious events thinking, and actually believing, that I needed to be more "spiritual." I needed a way to act out my faith on a daily basis, not just at organized gatherings that rarely fit me. I often left feeling that I was less spiritually connected than those around me.

Shudda: The old ways you were taught are the only way. There is no other way.

Cudda: You can just consider all other ways as blasphemy.

Wudda: And if everyone questioned faith as you do, can you imagine the chaos we would have in our churches?

IMAWISE: Asking yourself about your own spirituality leads to answers that make sense to you.

NEW THOUGHT

I ask questions about spirituality
in order to determine what
makes sense to me.

I heard the phrase, "Follow your bliss." I took it to mean, "Do whatever makes you happy." It took me a long time to realize that doing my right work in life was most likely the same thing as "following my bliss." When I entered a right relationship with the kind of work I do, I found blissful moments.

Shudda: What's all this talk about bliss? Just do what you are called by the Almighty to do.

Cudda: It is hopeless to try to find bliss. The best learning comes from suffering.

Wudda: What is unfair is how much suffering you have to endure to get a little happiness.

IMAWISE: Your bliss is the work you came here to do. You will know it once you have found it.

NEW THOUGHT

My right work is something I will
recognize. It will enliven me.

I was sure I could change everything. I tried, anyway, only to find that head-banging was uncomfortable. I honestly did not know that there are things one cannot change. Once I came to that understanding, I stopped trying so hard and began to relax.

Shudda: Only the Almighty can change certain situations.

Cudda: If you had used your faith more, you could understand that.

Wudda: There are dozens of reasons why certain things can't be changed.

IMAWISE: Once you know that change is not all up to you, you can relax.

NEW THOUGHT

I recognize that I cannot change all
things, and I no longer try.

Since childhood, I wanted to look like someone other than the face I saw in the mirror. Somehow the person in the mirror felt shame about her looks. Models, cousins and others were better off than I was in the looks category. That feeling lingers today, although I have mellowed some.

Shudda: If you are not grateful for what you have, you will lose your looks to some disease.

Cudda: Some disease or accident will befall you. Better find a way to be grateful.

Wudda: You have what you have because you came from your parents; what more can you expect?

IMAWISE: Let go of the need to compare yourself with others and find ways to use what has been given to you. You can be content.

NEW THOUGHT

I can let go of the need to be like others
and find contentment within myself.

I often left a task feeling as if I could have done more and should have done more. I thought of the things that were not done and might have been done if only we had thought of them in time. I rarely appreciated my efforts or the efforts of my partners.

Shudda: That's keeping on your toes.

Cudda: Staying on your toes will prevent the worst from happening.

Wudda: It's unfair that you are the only one who thinks of these things.

IMAWISE: It is good to appreciate your own efforts.

NEW THOUGHT

Today I enjoy and appreciate
my own efforts.

Anytime I feel confused, I often let that feeling become panic, and the panic overtakes me. I do not like confusion. It seems to spell impossibility at all levels, and it is hard to move forward from there. After years of this, I've found that confusion sometimes leads to clarity.

Shudda: When you're confused, you just can't think, so do something else.

Cudda: Don't make major decisions because they will be the death of you.

Wudda: Your confusion as a child has carried over into your adult life.

IMAWISE: Confusion can be the first step to clarity; it is a stopping point that gives you time to figure out your next step.

NEW THOUGHT

I can use my confusion to help me
determine my next step.

September 7

The natural wonders of this world amaze me. The "mittens" in northern Arizona, the natural bridge in Virginia. Rock and stone formations, animal and plant life dazzle me. Yet I make little time for enjoying them. At the same time, I do not want them on my list of regrets.

Shudda: The Almighty is a greater artist than any human will ever be.

Cudda: You need to try harder to see what you want to see.

Wudda: You would have the time except that your first job is to do your calling. If that seems unfair, you can just realize that someone has to do it.

IMAWISE: Enjoying natural beauty can be a real part of the rest of your life. You can do that every day.

NEW THOUGHT

I need only make time in each day for appreciating natural wonders.

I long to know more about animal and plant life. I have studied rock and rock formations. I want to know more about ecosystems and how we all work together to survive.

Shudda: Sounds like a lot of liberal talk to me!

Cudda: You could understand other species if you had studied to be a biologist, but that is not what you do.

Wudda: Nor was it what you were called to do.

IMAWISE: Understanding the roles of others in ecosystems will help you to understand your own.

NEW THOUGHT

Today, I try to see my role in the ecosystem around me. I know I am responsible for what I do.

I listen to others too much and lose sight of my own mission and desires. I think that most others know more about life, and my life in particular, than I do. I lose track and then get lost on my own path. I find my way back when I realize the folly of this move and that others do not hold my direction.

Shudda: Now wait a minute, dearie; others know more than we do.

Cudda: You could have tried harder to listen to them, to find out what they had to say.

Wudda: What would this world be like if everybody did what you want to do and listened only to themselves?

IMAWISE: The voice within is your guide. Everyone has this gift from the Creator. It is your choice to listen.

NEW THOUGHT

I choose to listen to the voice within
me for the guidance I need.

Not only do I jump in to handle other people's affairs, I dart in to save them from their mistakes. I think somehow that I know what is best for them before they do, and that they need me to be there in order to resolve their problems. I now realize that this is a tremendous energy drain on my creative resources, and I now let others learn from their mistakes.

Shudda: If you have the answers, you must help. Duty calls!

Cudda: What harm could you do in helping others when you know the answers? How could you turn them down?

Wudda: It's a tough job, but somebody's got to do it!

IMAWISE: Others need to learn from their mistakes. Haven't you learned a great deal from your own?

NEW THOUGHT

I can let others learn from
their mistakes.

I am unable to wait for most things. Friends have informed me that I am impatient. Others have offered to pray for patience for me. I am impatient most with my own concerns, and this seems to annoy others. I find waiting for anything I want nearly intolerable.

Shudda: Patience is a virtue you do not have.

Cudda: And you could have it if you'd only try harder. What if you just decided you could do it?

Wudda: I think it is almost impossible for you to wait for anything because it seems like whatever you want will never get here.

IMAWISE: You learn to wait one situation at a time. It is simply a choice you make each moment you live.

NEW THOUGHT

I choose how I will wait for anything.

Dreams were visions of other people's worlds. I wanted whatever they had. I especially wanted what others had if they appeared to be living their dreams in the real world. They seemed free and eager to do each day of their lives.

Shudda: Your dreams are too big. You can't do anything that big.

Cudda: What if everyone dreamed that big? Then nothing would ever get done, eh?

Wudda: You blow smoke too often, you know, just to impress other people. You are not a doer, you are a dreamer.

IMAWISE: Look at the dreams you have made come true. What steps did you take to make them happen?

NEW THOUGHT

If I choose to make my dreams real,
I can also figure out the steps
to reach them.

September 13

I discovered through dreams, reading and therapy that I have an inner child. I can now see her and talk with her. I still find, however, that I put her in the background much of the time. I know that I am healthier as an adult when I let her come out more.

Shudda: All this to-do about an inner child! I never had one and still don't.

Cudda: That's just a sneaky way of blaming your parents for your own problems.

Wudda: If you let her out more, assuming she really exists, then every decision takes more time. You are running out of time!

IMAWISE: It is healthy to learn about your inner child.

NEW THOUGHT

I choose to be a friend
to my inner child.

I find that my inner child needs are different from my needs as an adult. We share the same body, but I often minimize her basic needs. The result is that I feel her anger somewhere in my body, and I am dealing with it. I am doing the same thing to her that my parents did. She feels betrayed.

Shudda: Nonsense! You sound crazy!

Cudda: How could you make up for what your parents did not do?

Wudda: Just act like she's not there!

IMAWISE: She is the injured part of you, the injured who waits for your good care.

NEW THOUGHT

I learn to take good care of my inner
child moment by moment.

September 15

If I accept the feelings of my inner child, then the next logical step is to let her have a say in the decisions I make. This would be a way to assure her that I care about what she needs and that her needs will be continually considered.

Shudda: Now you've lost it! You've really gone overboard!

Cudda: Just exactly how could you explain this to your parents? What would you say—"I'm taking care of the little person you neglected"?

Wudda: This is impossible for you to do. You can't turn back the hands of time.

IMAWISE: It is not necessary to turn back the hands of time to right any wrong done to the inner child. Today, she needs your good care and consideration.

NEW THOUGHT

I consider the needs of my inner child
when I make any decision.

I've worked at many jobs, making a living as lifeguard, salesclerk, therapist, professor. All this time, I really believed I was doing what I *thought* I wanted to do at the time. Now I see that much of it was to impress others, especially my family. What did I love to do? What made me happy? I did not know.

Shudda: Now look, you were making lots of other people happy. Doesn't that mean anything?

Cudda: So many people needed you.

Wudda: Would you just let them go away empty-handed?

IMAWISE: When you find what makes your heart beat fast, you will also find the means to do it.

NEW THOUGHT

I can make a living from
what I love to do.

Where did I come up with the decisions I made? Once I made them, I found justification for them. Before I made them, I found no logic or understandable rationale for what later came out. Others said I was just emotional and over-reactive.

Shudda: Over-reactions get in the way and others don't like that. It looks silly.

Cudda: You need to care about how you look to others.

Wudda: Others have unjustly accused you without knowing your whole situation.

IMAWISE: Your decisions were the results of your best efforts at the time. It is good to honor your own efforts and the feelings you have.

NEW THOUGHT

I honor my own efforts
and my emotions.

Instead of trying to persuade others to accept my point of view, I find that I need to listen more intently to what they are saying. I am learning to listen and at the same time releasing the need to have them agree with me all the time.

Shudda: Ooooh! If you don't agree with others, they will turn on you.

Cudda: That could bring you down entirely; no job, no house, no friends, no food . . .

Wudda: Out on the streets—then what?

IMAWISE: Agreeing to disagree is a powerful healing tool. Listening to someone else tell his or her story is also.

NEW THOUGHT

Today I choose to listen to others.
I let go of the need to change them.

I know things by learning and by hunch or intuition. What I learn in school or in books or by experience is often wrong or doesn't hold up. Intuition is another thing altogether. It is rarely wrong and most often leads me to safety and satisfaction. I have come to believe it is a gift of the Creator.

Shudda: Women who use this are not to be trusted.

Cudda: Not to be trusted, not to be trusted! They are hopelessly selfish.

Wudda: You have to learn things through experience. There is no magic in your hunches.

IMAWISE: You know what you know. You know what you need to know when you need to know it. You can trust that.

NEW THOUGHT

My intuition and other ways of learning
are all powerful informants.

Lately I have been more in touch, moment to moment, with the things that give me joy. These things range from the tiniest speck to monolithic forms in the rolling plains near our house. This has opened up countless new worlds of interest and excitement for me.

Shudda: The Almighty is the maker of joy. Don't get sidetracked!

Cudda: You could get lost in these ideas and get real lazy.

Wudda: You can't take it all in anyway. There's just too much of it. Back to work!

IMAWISE: Taking in the things that bring you joy is a prayer of gratitude.

NEW THOUGHT

I choose to be grateful
all day long.

Looking for joy in each minute of the day sounds like work. I've found that I can do this simply by being thankful for what I have and looking for things to enjoy. So it doesn't really matter what I am doing as long as I have this attitude.

Shudda: God sends rain on the just and unjust. Don't get too happy. You'll get yours!

Cudda: If I could get you to hear one thing, it would be this: "Don't get too happy!"

Wudda: Just like hopes and dreams, this good mood you're in will come and go.

IMAWISE: There is joy in each minute when you remember your Source.

NEW THOUGHT

I face situations with joy and gratitude,
remembering my Source.

I have often shared too much of my life, and either trusted too much or too little. This combination has been deadly when I trusted the wrong persons. They often used the shared information to help themselves, against me and for their own gain.

Shudda: Loose lips sink ships. Need a life raft, dearie?

Cudda: This was easy and you made it hard. Just button the lips. Stop talking!

Wudda: No one, and I mean no one, really cares. So don't get the idea that you can get therapy from everyone you meet.

IMAWISE: Trust is built between people who have earned it.

NEW THOUGHT

I trust when I see that someone is
worthy of my trust. I share
myself when I can trust.

September 23

I shared my ideas in ways that left me unprotected. I saw no need to protect whatever project I was developing. I reasoned that no one would steal any idea because *I* would not steal an idea. That, I found, is not true. I am learning to protect what is important to me.

Shudda: Sounds verrry selfish to me!

Cudda: What do you have that others might want?

Wudda: This goes along with what I have been saying. Keep it all to yourself. No one can be trusted!

IMAWISE: Keeping your ideas private safeguards their power. When you have work to do, you are also in charge of the power around it.

NEW THOUGHT

Today, I choose to keep my ideas
private until I feel the time is
right to release them.

Early on in a conflict, I learned to give in and give up whatever was important to me. I learned that it went easier on me and I was safer if I did that. Today, I know that I had the right then to protect what was important to me. I back up my own decisions with action.

Shudda: So you are blaming your parents again? Do you have any idea how hard their lives were?

Cudda: Do you understand why they did what they did? They did the best they could.

Wudda: You do not honor them, so as a result, many things will feel impossible to you.

IMAWISE: You can learn ways to take care of what is important to you. You have that right.

NEW THOUGHT

I learn new ways to protect
my rights.

I did not feel that I had a right to a share of anything in the family in which I grew up. There was much talk and conflict between my parents over what was right for me. Rarely was I asked what I thought. They fought, and I did what they asked me to do. I learned from this to ignore my own feelings and to do what others wanted me to do.

Shudda: Your parents knew what was best for you. They always did.

Cudda: Right. This is the way that the Almighty meant for it to be.

Wudda: Leave it up to you, and you would have the children of the world telling the adults their needs!

IMAWISE: Healthy children are those who figure out what they need and let the adults live their own lives.

NEW THOUGHT

I am learning to guide my own life,
letting others do the same for themselves.

Because there was little *real* help early on, I learned to be very suspicious of those who offered it. I just knew they had a secret agenda, and I became skilled at figuring it out. Only problem was, at times they had no agenda other than kindness.

Shudda: I think you are bad-mouthing your parents again. Shame! Shame!

Cudda: They did the best they could and you are still complaining?

Wudda: So it was unfair. So what? Live with it and get a real life!

IMAWISE: It was hard to accept kindness. It gets easier when you practice kindness, beginning with being kind to yourself.

NEW THOUGHT

I am kind to myself no matter
what mood I am in.

When things were free, I thought they were basically worthless. I have found a gem in almost every community I have lived in, and that is the public library. Here is a free gem. I only wish I had spent and could spend more time in the libraries I have seen. These are great human-built wonders.

Shudda: You don't make enough use of free things. Always wanting to spend money!

Cudda: You could have learned this lesson long ago, now couldn't you?

Wudda: You just refused the good help sitting right there before you.

IMAWISE: The public library, like other free services, is a gift of the Creator, made possible by human efforts.

NEW THOUGHT

I look for gifts of the Creator that are there for my use and enjoyment, and made possible by others.

Things are not as serious as I have made them all these years. Laughter, and especially my own giggling, have seen me through some incredibly serious situations. I walked through terror more than once by finding something totally absurd about the event unfolding before me.

Shudda: Silly is as silly does!

Cudda: You could lighten up and there'd be less work for all of us.

Wudda: With all the sadness in the world around you, you really do not have time to lighten up.

IMAWISE: Laughter is healing. Your giggle is a gift of the Creator.

NEW THOUGHT

I still look for funny things and
find healing in this.

Laughter, oddly enough, helped me to see the difference between things I could change and things I could not change. For a long time, I did not know there was a difference.

Shudda: You can change all things by praying, if you just try.

Cudda: If you try hard enough, you can move the biggest mountain.

Wudda: You can't always depend on help from others. Just keep trying by yourself and with a lot of luck, maybe you'll make it.

IMAWISE: Knowing the difference between the things you can change and the things you cannot is a healthy step.

NEW THOUGHT

Today I take time to see what is mine
to change and mine to leave alone.
I find something humorous in
each situation I face.

I long for good health habits that only take three weeks of my life. I do not want to change my lifestyle. I want miracles of good health from minimal effort. In short, I think it could be said that I am lazy when it comes to my own health.

Shudda: Lazy is the devil's handmaiden!

Cudda: If you are lazy, you deserve what you get.

Wudda: You have to work very hard on your health all by yourself if you are going to live a long time.

IMAWISE: Good health habits are decisions made one at a time. The choices are yours—one at a time.

NEW THOUGHT

I will rethink my current habits and
take the road to good health,
one step at a time.

OCTOBER

Refusing to ask
for help means
I think I know all
I need to know.

October 1

For many years, I questioned my own beliefs only when they got me into trouble. In graduate school, I found a safe setting to look at my beliefs and to determine their origins. I found many of the things I believed were imposed on me as a child and that I had never taken the time to see if these beliefs still fit.

Shudda: What was taught to you as a child is the truth.

Cudda: If you buck all that you learned, you are really asking for it.

Wudda: It is unfair to think that you should question everything you learned as a child. Too scary!

IMAWISE: Questioning your beliefs feels threatening, and it helps you grow.

NEW THOUGHT

I examine my beliefs to see
what really fits me.

Now that I live in the mountainous West, near the plains, I see many birds of all kinds, especially hawks and eagles. They are fascinating. I wish now that I had taken the time to learn more about them and their ways. I want to understand their dual natures and their relationship to humans.

Shudda: This bird stuff should have been learned in grade school. Why do you need to do this now?

Cudda: You could have spent more time and shown more interest in biology.

Wudda: What good would it do you now to look into this stuff?

IMAWISE: The creatures of the air are treasures. Understanding them and their fates leads us to understanding our own.

NEW THOUGHT

My curiosity is a healthy part of me
that leads to understanding more
about myself and others.

October 3

I often think that the sheltered life is a sad life. As a sheltered younger person, I missed a number of adventures. It also makes me wish I had taken more chances and tried more things.

Shudda: Taking chances is just too risky. You need to pay attention to what you are supposed to do.

Cudda: Do you even have the slightest idea of the risk you'd be taking if you were to take more chances?

Wudda: Don't you think that life is risky enough?

IMAWISE: Taking chances is a risk and an opportunity to grow.

NEW THOUGHT

I now judge well the risk that I need to take to have the lifestyle I want.

I've always loved fall, from beginning to end. Fall in the Piedmont of Virginia is special; the colors take your breath away. The other seasons pale by comparison. Now, in looking back, each season brought its own news, worth listening to and being aware of. I long for the times when I could have paid more attention to this labor of Nature.

Shudda: The blessings of the Almighty just escape you, don't they?

Cudda: You could have chosen to pay more attention!

Wudda: What you don't cherish, you often lose; did you know that?

IMAWISE: When you are young, you learn to appreciate certain things. At other ages, you will learn to appreciate other things.

NEW THOUGHT

I appreciate the work of the Creator as it appears in the cycles of Nature.

October 5

Some people tell jokes well. I do not. Many people understand jokes more quickly than I do. It takes me awhile to "get" them. It leaves me with the idea that I am still too serious about life.

Shudda: You should be serious about life. Life is a serious deal, and you only get one go-around.

Cudda: If you get too silly, you do not know what could happen.

Wudda: Then what would you do? As soon as you begin to enjoy life too much, what you want will be taken out of your reach.

IMAWISE: There is a time to be serious and a time to laugh. You know which is which.

NEW THOUGHT

I can trust my reactions to
the events around me.

292

For many years, I wished I lived any other place than where I lived. I have lived in many regions of the United States and in all kinds of dwellings. If we lost the house that we have, we have a tepee to live in. It seems I have never fully appreciated the homes loaned to me until I left them.

Shudda: Now see, this is what I am talking about. Never grateful!

Cudda: It is hopeless to get you to see what you have been given.

Wudda: Others have so little, and look at what you ignore.

IMAWISE: It is important to offer thanks for any place where you live.

NEW THOUGHT

Today I choose to be grateful for
the house where I live.

October 7

I have been told that it is really my fault that I do not get my needs met. Others are not mind readers. In order to get what I need, I must figure it out and then make those needs known. This used to make me furious; now I see it as a way to take care of myself.

Shudda: Well, it doesn't really matter what you say. Other people have their own needs and they will take care of those first.

Cudda: If you start saying these things all the time, everyone will think you are nagging.

Wudda: And that won't work. Try it; others will get tired of you real soon.

IMAWISE: There is a calm and safe way to let others know what you need.

NEW THOUGHT

I can let others know what I need in a way that promotes getting my needs met.

I often stay inside on beautiful days and I do not know why. I just haven't let myself enjoy the gorgeous sunny days we often have in New Mexico and Wyoming. It is as if I think that the weather will stay this way and that there is plenty of time to be out in it. Also, I have not found the ways that I like to enjoy myself outside.

Shudda: You need fresh air. You need activity.

Cudda: While you are young, you need to enjoy being active as long as you can.

Wudda: What would you do if suddenly you couldn't go outside and enjoy the great weather?

IMAWISE: Some folks have to learn to enjoy themselves in different situations, especially if they have come from sheltered backgrounds.

NEW THOUGHT

I take the time to figure out what I might enjoy.

October 9

Married to my own opinion, I have often been afraid to leave it to examine other views. It seems that I felt threatened by ideas unlike mine. I couldn't look at other people's views, so I chose to blind myself to them. I now think that I missed a lot by choosing to stay stuck in my own opinions.

Shudda: When you're right, you're right. Right?

Cudda: You know others could just be stuck in their opinions and not want to hear yours.

Wudda: It is impossible to get others to listen and it is simply unfair that you should have to do all the "bending."

IMAWISE: It is important for your growth to learn to listen to the opinions of others and to share your own.

NEW THOUGHT

I can learn ways to share and
exchange opinions.

As a child I learned to use big words correctly most of the time. One day, a beloved teacher told me that I did not write very well. This was in the wake of accolades from many others who told me that I did write well. More than anything, I wanted to write. I struggled with the choice of whom I would believe.

Shudda: Teachers know best! Listen! That's why they are teachers.

Cudda: What if she told you that you could write and it wasn't true?

Wudda: If you really try hard to write, and what you write looks silly to someone like an editor, don't you think you will feel silly?

IMAWISE: You know in your heart what you want to do. You can choose what you think of your own ability.

NEW THOUGHT

I choose to believe in my ability.

Whenever I spent time with my family as a child, I ended up feeling hurt or left out. It was as if I wasn't there. I would then try even harder to get noticed, by being a clown or an entertainer, or the most educated on a subject of interest to the family. I still wish that I had found a way to have more quality time with my family.

Shudda: And well you should have. At least they didn't leave you all alone.

Cudda: What was it that you didn't try that could have made things better?

Wudda: They were dealing with really important things at that time, don't you see?

IMAWISE: Your feelings are normal and natural. There was nothing you needed to do differently with family members whose focus was on their own needs.

NEW THOUGHT

I forgive myself for the role
I played in my family.

Once I decided to learn all I could about families and human behavior, it freed me to look at the ills of all families, including my own. Once I began to study this, my own ways began to change. I wish now that I'd learned that sooner, so that all my young adult years could have been lived to the fullest.

Shudda: You can read all you want about families, but you have to do right by your own.

Cudda: You could have found a different way to be with your family.

Wudda: And it would have made a big difference, since you think it was so unfair to you.

IMAWISE: Studying about families helped you to learn what you needed. If you need that now, you can look to yourself to meet that need.

NEW THOUGHT

I no longer look to broken promises
of the past. I meet my own needs
in the best ways I know today.

I left home at 22 and tried to make a life for myself. It didn't work, and I wanted to return to get myself together. My family said no. I was faced with having to leave again and find a different way that pleased me more. Someone said to me, "You can never go home again." The hurt in my heart told me that that was true, at least for me.

Shudda: Forgive and forget!

Cudda: They probably couldn't help you anymore.

Wudda: You probably would still be there if they had let you stay.

IMAWISE: This was a confusing time that you chose to make the best of. You have learned how to make lemonade from some of life's lemons.

NEW THOUGHT

I can turn situations that hurt me
into ones that help me.

When I learned at age 11 that I could make money, and lots of it, I found a new power not available to me at home. I learned right away about buying power at this early age. I liked working hard because it was usually appreciated by others. Thus began two addictions in my life: overworking and overspending.

Shudda: Excess is the devil's friend.

Cudda: You could have waited to work and spend money. You didn't need all those things you bought.

Wudda: Since you felt there was no one there for you at home, it was easier to go elsewhere to find money and approval. Think of the childhood you missed.

IMAWISE: You learned some powerful lessons with this head start in the work world.

NEW THOUGHT

Today I pay close attention to my
excesses and look for the
reasons behind them.

Threats of any kind just shut me down. I leave this kind of situation quickly or give in to the person making the threat. This has always seemed to me to be the safest move. Today, though, I take time to understand what I find threatening. In this way, threats become my teachers about the boundaries I need to set for myself with others.

Shudda: If you are threatened, you are not using your faith.

Cudda: Right. And look what you could do if you used your faith.

Wudda: The reason you can't use your faith is because you always end up on the short end of the stick when you do.

IMAWISE: Threats of any kind teach you about the limits you need to set for yourself.

NEW THOUGHT

I can see threats as clues to help me
protect myself and my interests.

Each day passes and I spend little time, if any, on meditation. I pray during the day but have never developed a way or "the time" for meditation. I run from the moment I rise till the moment I hit the sack at night. I look back and wonder about the direction that the day might have taken if I had stopped to meditate.

Shudda: Pray! Pray! Meditation is for foreigners.

Cudda: A day without prayer is like a day without sunshine.

Wudda: Your day is likely to be impossible in all ways without this attention to meditation.

IMAWISE: You can choose the best time in your day to talk with your Higher Power. You know the right time.

NEW THOUGHT

I talk to my Higher Power during the day.
I choose the times that suit me best.

October 17

It is wonderful to walk and pay close attention to your surroundings. There are so many things that are missed when you move around by car or bike. Walking, it is said, is the best exercise for most folks and yet, I always put other things first.

Shudda: You should appreciate your ability to walk; someday you may not be able to do that.

Cudda: You could make it a priority every day—no matter what.

Wudda: Your schedule being as it is, is impossible. You can't really fit anything else into it.

IMAWISE: This is one good step for healthy living. You can choose to be disciplined about this or something that fits you better.

NEW THOUGHT

I can use the discipline that I apply to
other things to walking as well.

I like challenges. Most of the ones I have set for myself in the past have been outrageously tough, almost out of reach. I really bent and stretched myself and my resources to reach them. Now I look for challenges that can be reached in reasonable ways and in realistic time frames.

Shudda: Look at what you've done with your temple. Your body is a temple.

Cudda: If you took time to rest, you could reach the big challenges you really want.

Wudda: It is important to try the impossible and make it look easy.

IMAWISE: A challenge is a growth prospect. It can be reached one step at a time.

NEW THOUGHT

I can challenge myself in
reasonable ways.

October 19

I thought success was all that was important. Success was so important to me that to get it, I bent over backwards to please everyone I thought I needed to please. It did not work for one reason: I was not personally pleased with what I chose to do. I long for all the time that I spent trying to be like other people who are successful. I want that time back to reinvest in what pleases me.

Shudda: It looks to me like you've wasted an awful lot of time coveting other people's talents and experiences.

Cudda: You could have been thankful for what you had.

Wudda: Just think of all the time you missed working on your hopes and dreams.

IMAWISE: You can define success for yourself.

NEW THOUGHT

To define success for myself, I choose
the road that is important to me.

306

Terrified of failure, I spent much time worrying about when it would happen. Failure did happen, and I crashed. I made excuses that made sense to me. Still, I failed and I hated it. Once those feelings were put aside, I began to organize to succeed in this same endeavor.

Shudda: Can't you let well enough alone?

Cudda: If you had the ability to do this well, you could have succeeded in the first place.

Wudda: The reason you failed was because the person in charge did not like blonde-haired women.

IMAWISE: Failure is a teacher not much different from success. Our feelings about both are teachers also.

NEW THOUGHT

Today I let failure, success and
my feelings teach me.

I feel ashamed when I get a letter in the mail from a friend. I feel right away that I should be writing more letters and calling less. Then I hear that letter-writing is a dying art. If I had written more letters, I could have more contact with many friends from the past.

Shudda: See, *there's* something to do with all your free time.

Cudda: It's possible to do this if you plan your day just right.

Wudda: No one can help you with this one. It's up to you.

IMAWISE: This is a personal choice that means a real investment of time.

NEW THOUGHT

I choose to communicate with significant
others in ways that make sense
for my lifestyle.

I have long hated mistakes. I do not like to make them and learned early on that others like it better when you do not make them. I learned also that mistakes were shameful things that were of no value, things to be avoided at all costs.

Shudda: Now you're talking. Keep trying for perfection.

Cudda: If you follow the rules that they set, you can make few mistakes.

Wudda: What do "they" know, anyway? Is it fair to you to say you can never make a mistake?

IMAWISE: Mistakes are normal, natural events in human life. You are entitled to your own mistakes, and you can let them teach you.

NEW THOUGHT

I see the mistakes that
I make as friends.

When someone else received recognition, I rarely liked it, and felt somehow it meant that I was less than I needed to be. I needed attention so badly that I would do almost anything to get it. I believed that there wasn't enough attention to go around.

Shudda: Jealousy is a green giant that will eat you alive.

Cudda: Besides, when you cannot see that others need attention, too, you are being self-centered and selfish.

Wudda: If all the world had your response, what kind of mess would we be in?

IMAWISE: When you learn to pay attention to your talents and needs, it frees you to appreciate the same in others.

NEW THOUGHT

Today I appreciate talent in everyone, including myself.

I finally felt at peace in the high desert and I wondered if that feeling would last. I started out feeling that way, it seemed, in a number of places. Only later did I fall "out of love" with those same places. Still, this was home. A year later, I left it for an adventure with my partner in the wilderness.

Shudda: You just can't appreciate what you have.

Cudda: You could have tried harder to make it work in the place you loved.

Wudda: If you are ever going to get home, you will probably have to do it all alone.

IMAWISE: Where you live is still your choice. You can handle the consequences of your choice.

NEW THOUGHT

I know where I feel at home and I can choose to make my home there.

311

October 25

I want art in my life every day. I want to see it, be with it and be surrounded by it. I am amazed that this can happen naturally and almost daily with sunrises and sunsets here in Wyoming. It happened in New Mexico as well and in many other places where I've lived. Now I wish I had attended those daily "art shows." Now I spend time with the "Great Artist."

Shudda: I hope you are offering a prayer of thanks when you do it.

Cudda: This is something you could do every day if you made it a priority.

Wudda: Really, what would it take from you to appreciate this each day?

IMAWISE: Nature is the best art show around. You can take the time and use it for prayer or meditation if that fits what you need.

NEW THOUGHT

I appreciate the evidence of the Great Artist that is all around me in Nature.

There have been a number of people I needed to confront at one time or another and found it impossible to do. I still linger over the times when someone violated me and I did nothing to help myself. I still want to confront the person long after the fact.

Shudda: Revenge is the work of the devil.

Cudda: You could just let it go, forgive and forget.

Wudda: If you confront them, you will have to go alone, and that may be tough since you think they are so powerful.

IMAWISE: Confrontation may not may be possible at this time. It may not be the correct thing to do. See what you think about releasing the anger in another way.

NEW THOUGHT

I will look at freeing myself from anger.

Hope is a curious thing. I haven't had much of it in my 42 years. Even when things came out alright in the end, hope did not seem to have played a big role. I think I learned to be hopeless. It was a way to remain passive about things that bothered me.

Shudda: Hope is the beginning of faith. No wonder yours doesn't work.

Cudda: If you figure out why you have little hope, you can strive to get more of it in your life.

Wudda: If you would act on that, things would be going better right away.

IMAWISE: Hope is something you choose for yourself. It helps with your dreams and each moment you live.

NEW THOUGHT

Today I choose hope.

I could have had more hope if I'd had higher self-confidence or a sense that I could change things. I had to learn that I could do new things simply by trying. I was curious about what I could do and that helped me try new things.

Shudda: You can try too many way-out things, you know.

Cudda: That could get you in over your head, kid.

Wudda: What would you do then? Do you really think anyone would come to your rescue?

IMAWISE: Hope and self-confidence go hand-in-hand. One feeds the other. The two are a choice you can make.

NEW THOUGHT

I choose to have hope and self-confidence
as I make my way in the world.

When I first started doing what I wanted to do with my life, I really believed I needed much contact with the Muses, those guiding spirits of inspiration. I knew little about perspiration and hard work behind what I wanted to do. After a while, I found that inspiration comes with discipline and hard work.

Shudda: Hard work is good for the soul, but I wish you'd stay away from odd religions.

Cudda: You could just work harder and see what happens.

Wudda: Whatever you do, no one will do it for you. You will have to do it alone.

IMAWISE: Discipline and hard work are the legwork of all inspiration.

NEW THOUGHT

I do the legwork, and inspiration
springs from that.

I read to understand creativity. I thought if I could just get it in my head to understand creativity as a process, I could be more creative. Now I find I am more creative when I do not think so much about that.

Shudda: Do not hide your talents under a bushel basket.

Cudda: You need to use them to honor the Giver. That means using them in the right way.

Wudda: And if you want to use them in the right way, you need to study the experts and how they did it, before you try it alone.

IMAWISE: You are given gifts to use. You know instinctively how to make them grow.

NEW THOUGHT

I love my gifts and I practice
using them well.

I did not know that there was a wide arena in the world for people to try their own ideas. I heard a lot of people talk about doing that but saw few of them actually doing it. That showed me that it was awfully difficult to try your own ideas. Others told me that it was next to impossible. It was really scary when I began to try.

Shudda: O ye of little faith! Just believe!

Cudda: You needed to try harder; add more hours in your day.

Wudda: If you get them out of your way, you can actually get it done easier.

IMAWISE: There are many voices in the world that speak of what is possible. You must choose the ones you will hear.

NEW THOUGHT

For my ideas, I choose the
voice of possibilities.

NOVEMBER

For this one thing,
give thanks: the choice
to believe what you
want about yourself and
what you can do.

November 1

Finally in love and in a good relationship, I still find it hard to trust. In a place where it seems trust should come easy, I am left with only the feeling that I should be able to do better with it than I am doing.

Shudda: You haven't really trusted anyone ever, including your parents. What do you think the Almighty thinks of that?

Cudda: You could just try harder at it.

Wudda: The reason you can't do better is that you didn't trust as a child—and that is someone else's fault, not yours.

IMAWISE: Trust is something you build, and not all of us start with trust intact. You have started to learn trust from the ground up. Learn to appreciate where you are.

NEW THOUGHT

I can appreciate the steps I have taken
to trust others and work on the
next step as it comes up.

When I trust less than I need to, I am also left with the feeling that I have not loved as well as I should have. I feel I have let my partner down. This is often only my feeling, not his. Yet it is still there.

Shudda: You should trust and obey your partner's wishes if you are going to get along in this world.

Cudda: And you could get along better if you trusted the judgment of other people—experts you know.

Wudda: If you don't do what others say, you have no hope of reaching your dreams.

IMAWISE: The best you can do is all you can do.

NEW THOUGHT

I honor the efforts I make
in my relationships.

I guess I have perfected the art of nagging. I find all kinds of reasons to do it. I find that I am never satisfied with what I have done or another has done. It just isn't enough. It is never enough.

Shudda: Work, for the night is coming! Keep on keepin' on!

Cudda: What if everybody complained as much as you do?

Wudda: Why do you have to work so hard all the time? No one else seems to do that.

IMAWISE: There are ways to ask for what you want that are more productive than nagging. Try a new way.

NEW THOUGHT

I try new ways to ask for what I want.

I often find that I do not know what is important to my loved ones. I do not know because I do not listen, or do not ask, or simply reject their ideas in favor of something I thought to be more important.

Shudda: See here, dearie, this is where you lose it.

Cudda: You have no idea what will happen if you do this a lot.

Wudda: It is impossible to please everybody, and even the people you love change their minds a lot. So how can you win?

IMAWISE: You can study yourself to see what changes you need to make in this area.

NEW THOUGHT

I can change my relationships for the better when I look at my own behavior.

November 5

I am learning to take the time to find out what pleases those close to me. Early in my recovery, I found it hard to see what pleased me, but now that comes easier. I failed to see that others have preferences that are just as important to them as mine are to me.

Shudda: The most important thing you can do in life is please others.

Cudda: Right—a real must, even if they spit on you.

Wudda: I wouldn't go that far. That's not fair to you. Besides, some people are impossible.

IMAWISE: You can learn about what pleases you *and* others and work out a compromise.

NEW THOUGHT

When I learn to see what pleases me
and others, I can negotiate
in my relationships.

It took years for me to figure out what I really liked. I had to invest the time in each situation I faced to figure out what was attractive to me. This replaced my usual routine of just following the crowd or a trend set by someone else.

Shudda: You should pay attention to the experts. They know best.

Cudda: You need to try hard to stay one step ahead of the others. That's what people see and appreciate.

Wudda: You do not have enough money to be in the crowd, so learn to imitate them well.

IMAWISE: What pleases you also enhances your health and outlook.

NEW THOUGHT

I take time to make myself happy
in any situation I face.

I learned about the differences among people by traveling abroad. I looked at how others lived and found that all of us are amazing in our abilities to figure out what is handed to us in this life. Each of us is a gifted person.

Shudda: Now let's not go overboard. No one ever saw that in me.

Cudda: You could really go adrift here. Some differences in people cannot be respected.

Wudda: You can't really trust difference as much as you want to. Some differences can really hurt you.

IMAWISE: Differences make us rich. Differences give us a chance to grow in ways we cannot imagine.

NEW THOUGHT

I appreciate difference and look at how it can enhance my life.

When I first touched what was unique about myself, I was actually stunned. I did not know that there were unusual qualities about me that only a few others had. I felt joy, I think, and very unsure that this was really true.

Shudda: You have always ignored God's gifts to you.

Cudda: If you don't use them, you'll lose them!

Wudda: It's not fair to you if they are taken away before you can use them. Keep them hidden from others.

IMAWISE: You are given time to understand your own uniqueness. You are given time to develop it.

NEW THOUGHT

I am committed to understanding my unique gifts and using them well.

I have always been charmed by the uniqueness of others. Outstanding qualities of others fascinated me. This kept me from discovering my own talents. It led me also to an extreme sense of jealousy of what they could do. Again, I drifted from my own path.

Shudda: God sends gifts to many people who don't use them. They lose them!

Cudda: When you focus on what others can do, you forget that you have work to do and that you need to try harder to get yours done.

Wudda: If others do not see the uniqueness in you, it is because you have not shown them all you can do.

IMAWISE: When you appreciate your own gifts, you can let go of jealousy. You can appreciate others because their abilities take nothing from you.

NEW THOUGHT

I enjoy others' abilities.

I guess few people learn to trust their intuition early in life. I think we are all born with a very strong sense of what is right for us, but our social settings rob us of it. We learn not to listen to the voice within. I often wish now that I had learned to listen more to my intuition.

Shudda: Intuition is a troublemaker. Better listen to the experts.

Cudda: What if that were the only way you learned anything?

Wudda: Intuition is not to be trusted. Hard work on your own is the key, along with expert advice.

IMAWISE: You can make good use of intuition, expert advice and hard work.

NEW THOUGHT

I trust all of my faculties: intuition, hard work, and what I think about expert advice.

During any given day, I will look toward the sky. The sky in New Mexico and Wyoming is an ongoing pleasure; an artistic masterpiece. It is a forever changing mural that wraps the landscape in the prospect of things to come. I take the time to take in the clouds.

Shudda: This is a complete waste of time. This is time better spent working on something.

Cudda: You could daydream all day every day, and see where that gets you.

Wudda: This is a little crazy, isn't it? Your own dreams will float away on those clouds.

IMAWISE: A break in the day to feast on the beauty of Nature gives you a chance to feel grateful.

NEW THOUGHT

I will stop during my day to take in
the beauty of the natural world.

There is something really wonderful about being grateful. I experiment with this attitude from time to time. What I find is that I am very peaceful and joyful when I am grateful. I find that I accept easily what comes and I cannot be rattled in any situation.

Shudda: Well, it has certainly taken you long enough. Bet you can't stay there long!

Cudda: You could if you just tried harder to be more grateful.

Wudda: I would tell you that you can't always be grateful. Look how you grew up and what you lived through.

IMAWISE: Gratitude is a choice that leads to knowing you will be enough and have enough.

NEW THOUGHT

I choose gratitude.

I need to start each day by giving thanks. I forget that I want to do this. It really depends on what happened the night before and while I slept. It makes sense, though, to give thanks the first thing each morning.

Shudda: You should be giving thanks all the time.

Cudda: If you are not thankful for what you have, you are apt to lose it all.

Wudda: This is something no one else can do for you.

IMAWISE: Giving thanks is a wise way to begin the day. It is habit worth your time.

NEW THOUGHT

I can develop the habit of
gratitude by starting each day
with "Thank you."

I have heard that one is either creative or logical, not both. I do not believe that. I think that these abilities from each side of the brain can, and do, work together quite often. I've found that to be true several times as I worked on art projects. It does, however, take more effort for me to engage both sides.

Shudda: I am suspicious of the idea of two sides of the brain working together.

Cudda: It takes a lot of work to blend creativity and logic. I am not sure that it's possible for common persons like yourself.

Wudda: If you could do this on a regular basis, then everyone would do it, right?

IMAWISE: Everyone does use both sides of the brain to do many things. It is a wonderful cooperation we all have.

NEW THOUGHT

I look for ways to blend my
creative and logical sides.

I do not remember the Source of my ideas enough. Sometimes I get so lost in the idea that I forget the inspiration comes from a power greater than myself. I love the idea and forget to appreciate or give thanks for its origin.

Shudda: Now there's a spot of truth.

Cudda: If you forget the Almighty too often, your gifts will disappear!

Wudda: And then your dreams will go in that instant, too, dearie!

IMAWISE: It is important to remember the Source of all you do and need.

NEW THOUGHT

I give thanks for my Source.

There are times that I wish I had had biological children. I had stepchildren and that went well. It was a real blessing. I learned a great many things from them. I wonder what my own child might have been like. Then I look at my creativity in a similar way and appreciate that.

Shudda: One of the great sadnesses of your life: no children. Not a complete woman, are you?

Cudda: You could have had some if you had tried everything available to you to do that. You gave up too soon.

Wudda: It was really impossible for you to have children when you tried and now your biological clock says, "It's too late." Tough break, kid!

IMAWISE: Create what you love and love what you create.

NEW THOUGHT

I love what I create. I create what I love.

I walked away from talents I found I had early in life. I tried many things besides what I knew I had some ability to do. I used other talents to serve others and not to please myself. From there, I gained self-approval and pleasure from service to others.

Shudda: Serving others is the reason we are all here, right?

Cudda: That is the reason we can help each other—because it is our mission.

Wudda: But you can't always do this because there are not enough hours in the day. If you go to bed tired from serving others, your day has gone well.

IMAWISE: Serving others includes serving yourself well. Find a balance between the two.

NEW THOUGHT

I can find a balance between
serving self and others.

I am naturally curious. I think we all are. Few of us, however, feel good about asking questions or asking for help to understand what we want to know. I believe that I should already know things or that I have no right to interrupt others to get a better understanding of something. What often follows is an apologetic attitude just for "wanting to know."

Shudda: Pick the right time to ask and then excuse yourself when you are asking.

Cudda: You can't know all you need to know without asking others, so ask what you need to ask, no matter what the situation.

Wudda: Or just learn it all on your own. You ask for too much help, anyway.

IMAWISE: Asking questions and asking for help is normal human behavior. It reminds us that we need each other.

NEW THOUGHT

When I need help, I ask for it. I let myself feel good about my own curiosity.

Ugh! Compliments! What do you do with them? In the past, they have made me feel uncomfortable, uneasy, and sure the person saying them had a hidden agenda. I feared that the person wanted something from me, and sometimes he or she did. Honest compliments, however, were hard to deal with when I felt poorly about myself.

Shudda: Better take them when you can get them!

Cudda: When someone says something nice, nine times out of 10, they do want something.

Wudda: They see good things about you and they point them out just to help themselves.

IMAWISE: Say "Thank you" for any compliment and let it go at that.

NEW THOUGHT

I am learning to accept compliments,
letting them come and go.

In these early years of recovery, I am so self-absorbed. I am in the process of discovering myself for the first time, so naturally I am taken up with this process. It doesn't seem like that, until I realize that I have shut out the needs of others.

Shudda: Shame, shame! Forgetting others! Do you know where that will get you?

Cudda: You keep that up and the worst things will come to you.

Wudda: What you put out will most certainly come back to you a thousandfold.

IMAWISE: In the beginning of recovery, it was necessary to study yourself. As you go on, you can tune into the needs of others and still be aware of your own.

NEW THOUGHT

I am aware of my needs and the
needs of others as I recover.

I never thought it was okay to change my mind about something that seemed settled to everyone else. Others' strong reactions usually made me think that it was better to go along with decisions I had made than to balk and change them.

Shudda: Just go along with others—life is easier.

Cudda: If you stop everyone in midstream, you will be known as a troublemaker.

Wudda: And you will also be known as someone who is impossible to work with.

IMAWISE: If you change your mind, decide also that you can accept consequences and the reactions of others.

NEW THOUGHT

I can change my mind when I feel
it is right. I can also deal
with what follows.

If changing my mind was difficult for me, the decision to change my name was next to impossible. I did so only after long deliberation and meditation. Long uncomfortable with my birth name, I chose my own.

Shudda: You should honor your parents by keeping the name they gave you.

Cudda: You could have found a way to do that and chosen a nickname.

Wudda: You can't expect your parents, or anyone else, to get used to some new name you want.

IMAWISE: A name is what you walk behind. It is important to be proud of what you are called.

NEW THOUGHT

I choose what I am called.
It fits who I am.

I found that other people do not know my limits. I thought they did or that they could automatically figure them out. I did not think I had any responsibility for letting others know what I could and could not do.

Shudda: Setting limits means that you are growing selfish.

Cudda: You could bend a little bit here and there, if you weren't so rigid.

Wudda: The reason you can't have limits—real ones, that is—is because someone may need you when you least expect it.

IMAWISE: Get to know your limits and let others know them, too. You are healthy if you know and share your limits.

NEW THOUGHT

I am learning my limits and taking care to inform others of those limits.

I am reluctant to change my routine, even when it doesn't really work. I think I like ruts, at least the ones that I know well. When all the clues say "Change," I am slow to think about it and even slower in doing it.

Shudda: Changing slowly is good only if experts think it is a good idea.

Cudda: When the routine doesn't work, you have to change it right away or lose valuable time.

Wudda: If the routine you know doesn't work, it is usually because someone else got in the way.

IMAWISE: As you change, your routine will naturally change at the pace that is right for you.

NEW THOUGHT

I change my daily routine at
the pace that fits me.

When I talk to younger people, I find that they are not so hopeful about their own futures. Some have high levels of self-confidence and many do not. Many are struggling with the idea of liking themselves and learning to follow their own lead. They look for role models worthy to follow. If I could give them one thing, it would be hope.

Shudda: Younger people need to first listen to and honor their parents.

Cudda: They will find all the excuses in the world not to do that.

Wudda: The problem is all the crap in the media that these folks listen to, which of course, if you remember, you did, too.

IMAWISE: You can offer hope to younger people in the form of encouragement. It is the same gift you needed.

NEW THOUGHT

I offer encouragement to others.

When I opened myself to see lessons in all the situations I faced, I found lots of wisdom. This wisdom felt very personal and not applicable to others. When I talked about this with others, I found that they were facing the same things. I found I was not alone and wished for ways to share what I discovered.

Shudda: When you know the right way, you are obligated to teach it to others.

Cudda: You just have to learn to be convincing enough so they will listen.

Wudda: It would be good if you could spend your life convincing people that you know "the way."

IMAWISE: Sharing what you are learning is different from convincing others to follow you. There is great joy in discovering your own way.

NEW THOUGHT

I share what I am learning and let go of
the need for others to be like me.

November 27

I am beginning to trust that it is possible to have good relationships even if you come from a dysfunctional family, as I did. For a long time I believed that it was just not possible. Now I realize that I can learn better ways of relating than I once knew. These new ways make for better relationships all around.

Shudda: Your parents and family are not to blame for your poor relationships.

Cudda: That's right. They had their own problems.

Wudda: You were too much for them to deal with on top of all those problems.

IMAWISE: Being willing to learn new ways of relating is the key to good relationships.

NEW THOUGHT

I choose to find new and better
ways to relate to others.

I try to plan all my waking time. I like useful moments and dislike moments that are unplanned or free. I have few of these. Then I discovered the idea that unplanned time is often a healthy break from the usual routine. I also think it may indicate that I can trust that things won't fall apart if I stop working on them for a little while.

Shudda: If you fail to plan, you plan to fail. Idle time is devil's time!

Cudda: You only have so many minutes in the day! Pretty soon you will be whiling them all away.

Wudda: If everyone gave up their plans and just drifted along the way you are talking about, what do you think would happen?

IMAWISE: Plans and free time are healthy when used in a balanced way.

NEW THOUGHT

I can use plans and free time
in a balanced way.

I look at my partner and wonder if I am giving enough to him. Though he rarely complains, I find that I am still so self-centered and self-absorbed that I lose focus on him from time to time.

Shudda: That's a marriage killer! Just watch out!

Cudda: This is not an area where you can afford to make a lot of mistakes.

Wudda: Many people would leave you if you made this mistake once too often.

IMAWISE: You can lose touch and make mistakes in relationships, and find a way to recover from both.

NEW THOUGHT

When I lose touch with my partner,
I admit it as soon as I can and
try to make amends.

All this worrying! No way to relax. I am not worth my salt if I am not thinking about what needs to be done next. I saw this way of living nearly kill my father. I look for ways and times to relax during my day.

Shudda: Idle time gets you in trouble. Stay on your toes, dearie!

Cudda: You could overdo the break time too, you know!

Wudda: If you stop a lot, you will lose your momentum. Then you will have to start all over again. You will have to come from behind—even catch up!

IMAWISE: There is no race. Hurry is an illusion.

NEW THOUGHT

I can slow down, take a break and
find a working pace that is
healthy for me.

DECEMBER

Even the best plans
are subject to:

- change,
- rearrangement,
- failure,
- success,
- divine interruption.

December 1

As a young person, and still today, I watch TV for persons and ideas that I admire. I learned early on, though, that how others look was very important, even crucial. I learned that about myself, too. The problem with that was that appearance became the driving force for most of my energy.

Shudda: It's what is on the inside that counts, and once again you headed off in a terrible direction.

Cudda: You have to make the most of the gifts you have been given and still try to look good all the time.

Wudda: Yes, what would others think if you were overweight and sloppy? They would think something was wrong with you.

IMAWISE: You can learn to love your body without going overboard. Say loving things to your body and see the changes it creates.

NEW THOUGHT

Today I treat my body with respect in
my thoughts, words and actions.

After turning 30, I began to worry about my age. I began to think about old age and how I would want that part of my life to be. I thought about all the things I wanted to do before that time in my life. I studied the lines in my face and the condition of my body. I still made few changes in how I acted toward myself.

Shudda: Thinking and doing are two very different things.

Cudda: You could have thought of all this earlier and made better plans.

Wudda: Aging is one thing that you do not want to do alone.

IMAWISE: See the value of each season in your life.

NEW THOUGHT

I value highly each day and
season of my life.

December 3

I look back on the birthdays I spent working for someone else and believed I was enjoying myself. I wonder now what took me so long to figure out what it meant to enjoy myself. I wonder why it took me so long to enjoy each birthday.

Shudda: Still not very grateful, are we?

Cudda: What do you expect from someone who needs a crutch to explain all her behaviors?

Wudda: And who refuses to listen to what would make life easier?

IMAWISE: You are recovering from the belief that life is not enjoyable. You are finding the ways that you enjoy yourself.

NEW THOUGHT

I learn each day about the things
that bring me joy.

There are many things that I have deeply resented over the years. I believe that such resentments cause emotional problems and health problems, and still it did not matter. It felt better to hold onto a list of wrongs and wrongdoers.

Shudda: That is *not* love. You are investing in hate.

Cudda: You can do better than that. Forgive and forget.

Wudda: When others violate you, you think that you must be able to teach them something about how to treat you.

IMAWISE: Resentment ties you up. Find the boundary that was injured and decide now how you will protect it. As you can, let the resentment go—for your good.

NEW THOUGHT

I choose to let go of resentment and protect myself in ways that honor my limits.

If I let resentments go, it seemed that I would forget what hurt me, and that made it likely to happen again. I actually thought it would hurt me more to forget the violations of others. Forgiveness only meant others could hurt me again.

Shudda: Forgive and forget! That is the only thing to do here.

Cudda: When you remember what was done, then it is not forgiven and you are in the wrong.

Wudda: If you hold on to these bitter feelings, the things you want in life will *not* come to you.

IMAWISE: Letting go of bitter feelings and finding forgiveness will free you.

NEW THOUGHT

I let go of bitterness and choose forgiveness to free myself.

Coming out of a sheltered life that was directed by others, I found it very difficult to make exciting plans and then carry them out from start to finish. I did a lot of talking about such plans, rarely carrying them through. Then when I snorkeled in Hanama Bay in Hawaii, the sheltered life was over. Life opened up and became one exciting adventure.

Shudda: Now don't go wild on us here. Foreigners are dangerous to Americans.

Cudda: You could lose control easily and never have a business-like attitude again.

Wudda: What else could you expect from someone who had a very painful childhood? You may go overboard.

IMAWISE: Life is the adventure that you make it—one day at a time.

NEW THOUGHT

I choose how I will view my life. I make the most of what is given to me.

Once I found that my roots were in Ireland and Scotland, I wanted to see the homes of my ancestors. Having been disconnected for so long from my own traditions, this felt new and good. I knew and understood for the first time parts of myself that arise from culture and history.

Shudda: Time to appreciate the old ones.

Cudda: You have had no interest up to this point. What has brought this on?

Wudda: This is something that will take up all your time if you let it.

IMAWISE: Knowing your roots leads to more self-understanding.

NEW THOUGHT

I acknowledge the importance of
knowing my past and culture.

I know little about Irish traditions and history. I have not traveled there. I want to feel a connection when I do finally see the homeland of my ancestors. I long for a healthy connection with the past and cultural tradition. As others have that information for themselves, I feel a need for a similar connection to my own heritage.

Shudda: You should have thought about this when your parents made that information available to you.

Cudda: You could have, but you did not see this as important or related to you in any way.

Wudda: Now if you want to know about it, you will have to find it on your own.

IMAWISE: A healthy connection to tradition and one's culture is an important part of understanding the self.

NEW THOUGHT

I connect with tradition and my cultural heritage in ways that are pleasing to me.

December 9

I have done other people's bidding far too long. Now I am in the business of finding what makes my heart beat fast—*my* real passions. Once I started looking, it took no time at all to begin to find them.

Shudda: You should be paying attention to the good you can do for others.

Cudda: Service is first—service to others. This stuff about passion will only get you in trouble.

Wudda: If you get into finding this passion of yours, you'll be in it all alone.

IMAWISE: Your passions make you come fully alive.

NEW THOUGHT

I am coming fully alive when I find
and pursue my passions.

As I find what makes my heart beat fast, I need much more compassion for myself and my inner child than I have ever allowed. I know that I have given others much compassion over the years. Now it seems that it is my turn.

Shudda: If you love yourself too much, you will forget about loving others.

Cudda: You could get lost trying to have compassion for yourself. Serving others is where it's at!

Wudda: As far as your inner child goes, you are now a grown person. Let it go already!

IMAWISE: You do need compassion for yourself and for others. Practice this daily.

NEW THOUGHT

I choose the same compassion for
myself as I offer to others.

December 11

Having lived in many places, I've made a number of friends over the years. Very few do I still see and know. Recently, I saw an old friend on a television commercial, and I longed to visit her and others who had shared kind and lovely moments with me.

Shudda: You have work to do now and have little time to see or be with old friends.

Cudda: Service to others is the key, not looking back and wishing.

Wudda: If you spend a lot of time doing this, you will feel left out and then lose time on all your projects.

IMAWISE: It is a good thing to count your years in terms of the good friends you have known.

NEW THOUGHT

I remember my friends from past years
as blessings of the Creator.

I have listened to the problems of friends as long as I can remember. Early on, I was everybody's counselor. It worked well for us all. In most recent years, I spent much less time listening to the aches of friends. I wish now that I had given more time to this, as we soon parted and there was precious little time for friendship after that.

Shudda: See, you should have done it when you had the chance.
Cudda: You could still do it if you made your work in serving others your priority in life.
Wudda: It is really impossible to recapture that time, so just give it up as a mistake that you won't make again.

IMAWISE: You did the best you could for each of these friends. If you need to make changes, you can do that now.

NEW THOUGHT

I still create the relationships that I want.

December 13

My partner often reminds me that I think too much about everything. He says that I analyze things too much. He advises me to take vacations from all those thoughts during the day and let my mind drift.

Shudda: Idle thoughts are the devil's workshop! Devil's work!

Cudda: Something awful could happen while your mind is drifting.

Wudda: Then you'd have no one to blame but yourself. You can't really do this because there is so much work to do.

IMAWISE: Taking a break from any excess is a good idea.

NEW THOUGHT

I can just "be."

December 14

Always on the go, I don't want to miss anything. I will hold up till the eleventh hour just to see if anything happens. I have always found it hard to rest, as if when my eyes close, the real action will take place.

Shudda: The body needs rest, and you are not taking proper care of the gift given to you.

Cudda: You could make this a priority or catch up on it all at once.

Wudda: That would work, except you would get behind in your schedule.

IMAWISE: Rest is a necessity and it makes the other parts of your life go better. Besides, you do not want to miss dreams and their information.

NEW THOUGHT

I choose to rest my body when
I feel the need.

Finding the right gift for someone is a joy. I can see the person's face as she or he opens it. I can see the sense that I have understood what is important in the life of that person. More than that, when the gift fits, there is a solid connection between that person and me that feels good. I try to give all year 'round for that reason.

Shudda: Giving is the only way you will be happy.

Cudda: Giving and service, giving and service!

Wudda: You can't be giving all the time—who does that for you? No one!

IMAWISE: Giving and receiving make solid healthy connections.

NEW THOUGHT

I am open to the blessings that come
with giving and receiving.

It seems to me that I have zoomed through life and that it has zoomed by me. Slowing down was not an option. Often I wasn't even aware that I was going fast at all until complete exhaustion or sickness took over to remind me. Now I think of slowing down just to catch things I might miss.

Shudda: Work, for the night is coming!

Cudda: You could lose a lot of valuable time if you slow down too much. You do need to rest so that you can continue to work hard.

Wudda: You haven't been able to slow down because there is so much work to be done to help other people.

IMAWISE: Slowing down helps you to see all things in a richer, deeper perspective.

NEW THOUGHT

Slowing down helps my health and
the ways in which I relate
to my environment.

December 17

Slowing down would have meant that I had stopped long enough to enjoy more things. I wish I had learned and enjoyed more music over the years. I take precious little time for it now. When I do find the time, I use it to relax a weary body instead of exploring music for the sake of personal pleasure.

Shudda: Still, you can use music to serve others and learn about it that way.

Cudda: You could find a way to use it in your work and then you wouldn't have to miss it.

Wudda: There is time to discover the kind of music that would be useful in the work you do.

IMAWISE: Music can be useful; it can also be enjoyed for its own value.

NEW THOUGHT

I can choose to explore the things that interest me. Not all of them have to be connected with work.

The word "No" is a hard one. It is hard for me to say without qualifying it or offering reasons why I said it. I want anyone who hears that from me to be satisfied that "No" is the right answer and that it is understandable.

Shudda: You have to be careful with who hears "No" from you.

Cudda: You can't just say "No" without explaining yourself. What will other people say?

Wudda: If I said "No," I sure would have a good explanation for why I was saying it.

IMAWISE: You can say "No" when you need to; it is as simple as that. People have heard that word before and have lived through it.

NEW THOUGHT

I let others have their own reactions
when they hear "No" from me.

December 19

I feel really good in certain colors and depressed in others. I began wearing the colors that enhance my outlook several years ago, and still today they have the same effect. I pay attention to what calms me and is comfortable.

Shudda: That is nonsense! How can a color do that?

Cudda: I suppose you think it is important to spend money on the colors that calm you?

Wudda: If you are not calm, it is because of the interruptions in your life, not because of the colors you wear.

IMAWISE: Colors have certain vibrations and intensity. Choosing the ones that soothe is healthy.

NEW THOUGHT

I choose colors and clothing
that soothe me.

I often feel lost in Nature, as if I am not a part of it. I get out in the woods and love being there. I also have the feeling that Mother Nature is so much more powerful than I, she overwhelms me. I know that I am a part of that world and just need to relax in its presence.

Shudda: Do not worship Nature. That is not proper.

Cudda: You could spend more time in the wild if you weren't working all the time.

Wudda: What would you learn there that you can't learn from reading, or in some other place?

IMAWISE: You are a part of Nature and it takes time to understand your place in her systems.

NEW THOUGHT

I place a priority on finding my role in
the system of Nature around me.

I am learning that it is healthy to be my own best friend. It makes good sense because no one knows me as well as I do, and no one is likely to know what I want more than I do. And most important, no one is likely to care for my boundaries better than I can. I'm still learning.

Shudda: If you are so self-absorbed, won't others think you are just selfish?

Cudda: What if everybody did this? Who would be there for anyone else?

Wudda: You didn't have many friends early on, so I guess you are the only one available for you.

IMAWISE: Being your own best friend is the first healthy step you can take to being in good relationship with others.

NEW THOUGHT

I choose to be my own
best friend.

I think "kind" is the way to be these days; kind toward everybody. It just makes sense. I've always thought that and pretty much offered that to others—most others, except to myself. I left myself out and then felt bad. I was not aware that the very kindness I showed to others was exactly what I needed myself—in huge doses.

Shudda: Kindness is as kindness does.

Cudda: If you are so wrapped up in yourself all the time, I think others will just leave you alone.

Wudda: If this is all you can think about, then there is not much room for the work you came to do.

IMAWISE: Kindness to you and to others is the work you came to do.

NEW THOUGHT

I choose kindness today.

One regret I carry daily is that I never developed an interest in cooking. I cook rarely, and when I do, it is because I *have* to do it. When it is necessary, I can do it well, especially if I turn the food into artwork.

Shudda: Now this is something that you should have learned as a child.

Cudda: You could have paid more attention to things like this—the important things, you know.

Wudda: Well, there was really no one there to teach you, right? So how would know what to do?

IMAWISE: You can choose whether or not you want to learn skills you may have missed as a child.

NEW THOUGHT

I can learn anything I think
I missed as a child.

Over the holidays I find good places to eat and like many people, I overeat. I can put on five pounds each season without a thought. Walking through a kitchen, I can feast my eyes on something and pick up a pound. I often wish I could eat in moderation.

Shudda: Moderation in everything is the key, but what does a little overeating during the holidays hurt?

Cudda: What if everybody worried as much as you do about a little extra weight?

Wudda: You can always lose it later. Loosen up!

IMAWISE: Moderate eating may be a new idea for you. You can choose to sample everything, eat slowly and savor each taste.

NEW THOUGHT

Today I can eat more slowly
and savor what I taste.

December 25

I am constantly tapping my foot and wringing my hands when I must wait for something to happen. Patience is not my strong suit. I probably won't change this. Waiting can be miserable.

Shudda: Patience is not your virtue. You are always in a hurry.

Cudda: If you had patience in any measure, you could live a longer life.

Wudda: Then you would not have to worry like you do. You would have more time to get things done.

IMAWISE: Patience is something you practice by choice.

NEW THOUGHT

When I choose not to be patient,
I choose the consequences
that go along with it.

After years of thinking that "I am not enough" or "I do not have enough," it is really difficult to reverse that thinking. If I accept that "I am enough" and "I have enough" of whatever, then I have a whole lot of free time on my hands, previously given to worry.

Shudda: This is your lack of faith, plain and simple.

Cudda: And you could reverse this anytime you want to, but you prefer to worry instead.

Wudda: Your life would be so much better if you would stop all that worry and just try to fix things on your own.

IMAWISE: Practice saying "I am enough" and "I have enough" and see how that feels. See what it does to your day.

NEW THOUGHT

Today I choose to believe that there is enough of everything.

If I accept that I am enough and there is enough of whatever is needed by any of us, then I have to accept that my contribution to any endeavor is also enough. Accepting that means that I am, once and for all, "good enough."

Shudda: Isn't that what I've been telling you for years? The Creator doesn't make junk.

Cudda: Right, but you have found all these ways not to listen.

Wudda: You have convinced yourself that the opposite is true, since you think your family did not like you.

IMAWISE: Others' opinions often mask hidden feelings. Do not be fooled. Each of us, including you, is a gift of the Creator, full and whole.

NEW THOUGHT

I see myself as a gift.

I think from now on I will look into more ways to relax and enjoy all that is around me. Maybe I will eat more good food, take more naps or walks, or find other things that soothe me. I will look at ways to de-stress and actually try them.

Shudda: See, you have to rest that body so it is ready for service to others.

Cudda: You are probably still hopeless in this area. I won't put any money on you changing.

Wudda: You will have to refuse to do some things in order to get this rest you say you need.

IMAWISE: Good food, naps, rest, soothing things and ways to de-stress—ah, the essence of health!

NEW THOUGHT

I choose new ways
to strengthen my health.

December 29

One thing that brings me great joy and calm is to sit with our dog and cat. I watch them as they relax, and they do that for most of their day. I am amazed that what makes up their whole day is also what I find so hard to do. Sitting with them means I will still myself long enough for a brief and needed rest, and enjoy their company.

Shudda: These breaks are really hard to take, with all the housework there is to do around you.

Cudda: If you do too much of this, you will get lazy and nothing will get done.

Wudda: Too much of this sitting around will make you soft—you will forget what really needs to be done.

IMAWISE: Enjoying the company of others is a great pleasure, not to be missed in life.

NEW THOUGHT

I spend time each day with
family and friends.

The end of another year brings on thoughts of my need to be with and appreciate my loved ones more. This begins with loving myself, my inner child and my partner in a way that is comforting. It means making home a haven where help and honor are always available—for all beings who live here.

Shudda: You should love them while you can.

Cudda: You could lose them at any moment. So appreciate them while you have them.

Wudda: You, and only you, have to appreciate those people you love. If you do not love them enough, you are very likely to lose them.

IMAWISE: Loving is a process you learn by doing. There is no need to know it all now. You learn how to love as you go.

NEW THOUGHT

I learn to love others by practicing every day.

Staying in touch with my sense of a Higher Power—that seems to be the key. Feeling the presence of this Power, calling on It when I need It, is what I must do. I must remember the Source—All That Is. The Source is always available to me.

Shudda: If you act right and use it for the right things.

Cudda: You could lose that right if you misuse your connection to that Power.

Wudda: Then, of course, only the worst things in life would visit you.

IMAWISE: You can fully trust your connection to All That Is.

NEW THOUGHT

I can fully trust the gift of myself
and my connection to the
Source of the gift.